Six Inches Deeper

The Disappearance of Hellen Hanks

MERCER UNIVERSITY PRESS

Endowed by

TOM WATSON BROWN
and
THE WATSON-BROWN FOUNDATION, INC.

SIX INCHES DEEPER

The Disappearance of Hellen Hanks

A True Account of One of Georgia's Most Horrific Crimes

William Rawlings

MERCER UNIVERSITY PRESS
Macon, Georgia
2020

MUP/ P599

Published by Mercer University Press
1501 Mercer University Drive
Macon, Georgia 31207

9 8 7 6 5 4 3 2 1

Books published by Mercer University Press are printed on acid-free paper that meets the requirements of the American National Standard for Information Sciences—Permanence of Paper for Printed Library Materials.

Printed and bound in Canada.

This book is set in Adobe Garamond Pro.

Cover/jacket design by Burt&Burt

ISBN 978-0-88146-733-8
Cataloging-in-Publication Data is available from the Library of Congress

res ipsa loquitur

Also by William Rawlings

The Lazard Legacy (2003)

The Rutherford Cipher (2004)

The Tate Revenge (2005)

Crossword (2006)

The Mile High Club (2009)

A Killing on Ring Jaw Bluff
(Mercer University Press, 2013)

The Second Coming of the Invisible Empire
(Mercer University Press, 2016)

The Strange Journey of the Confederate Constitution
(Mercer University Press, 2017)

The Girl with Kaleidoscope Eyes
(Mercer University Press, 2019)

Contents

Preface

The murder of Hellen Hanks was a tragedy. It was a horrific crime, the needless, wanton taking of the life of an innocent woman, a thirty-four-year-old mother of three young children, and the subsequent dismemberment and burial of her body. As far as most of the world knew, she simply disappeared one day in August 1972, robbing her husband and family of a wife and mother, plunging them into a world of uncertainty as to her whereabouts and fate. The chance discovery of Hellen's remains some eight years later marked the beginning of a legal saga that would last for decades.

The man accused of Hellen Hanks's murder was the scion of a wealthy and prominent family in his hometown of Valdosta, Georgia, where the murder took place. His family's affluence allowed him to hire attorneys who were among the best of the best, pitted against the limited resources of a rural, south Georgia district attorney and the local investigative team. From a literary perspective, the tale is one of the ultimate sin, murder, as well as secrets and lies, arrogance, sex, race, the struggle between the haves and the have-nots, and, eventually, justice.

The January 1982 trial of the accused murderer, Keller Wilcox, was extensively covered by local and regional media. An excerpt from an article in the *Atlanta Constitution* is illustrative of the sensational nature of the proceedings:

> *A rich, handsome young married man from a prominent family is on trial here for murder. He's accused of killing his attractive secretary nearly a decade ago, cutting off her legs so her body would fit in a makeshift coffin, then burying her at night with the help of his aging father and two trusted black employees. He's defended by one of the most colorful—and respected—lawyers in the country. Prosecutors hint at a sexual motive. Defense lawyers say police threatened black witnesses with lynching and damnation to get confessions. The defendant's pretty, dark-haired former wife says on the stand that she was*

hypnotized by lawmen. A deaf-and-mute friend of the victim testifies that, shortly before her disappearance, the woman expressed fear of the man now accused of killing her.[1]

From a legal perspective, the case involves a number of thorny issues, including the sufficiency of circumstantial evidence and the admission of the testimony of vital witnesses who had been harshly interrogated, to name two. In the years following Keller Wilcox's conviction, appeals of his case would span the full gamut of the state and federal appeals court system.

The bizarre nature of the murder and the subsequent trial attracted not only newspaper coverage, but other media coverage as well. The November 1983 issue of *True Detective* magazine reported the case under the garish title of "Blood Rage of the Too-Passionate Groper!" In 1986, *Southern* magazine reported on "The Second Life of Keller Wilcox" when he was out of prison on an appeal bond. David Hanks, Hellen's son, penned a *roman à clef* titled *The Disappearance*, based on his mother's murder, as did Lamar Cole's son, David Cole, writing under the nom de plume of Daktoriano Rhoshambianski. *Investigation Discovery with Paula Zahn* featured the case in a November 2015 televised episode.[2]

The story is admittedly a complex one, beginning with the disappearance of Hellen Hanks on August 31, 1972, followed by the discovery of her skeletal remains in November 1980, and the trial of Keller Wilcox in January 1982. There were multiple court appeals through 1987 and multiple efforts to secure parole for Wilcox in the years that followed. He was finally released on parole in May 2008. The last action of the parole board in his case (as of this writing) took place in June 2017.

---

[1] *Atlanta Constitution*, January 11, 1982.

[2] https://m.youtube.com/watch?v=eID2I9gXVLY.

In writing this story, I have adopted a chronological approach, recounting perspectives and events as they happened over time. My goal has been to stick to the facts, avoiding speculation and the many rumors that circulated during the years Hellen Hanks was missing and the years of legal wrangling that followed. I have simply tried to present a true tale, truthfully told. The astute reader may note some occasional inconsistency in various "facts" in the narrative. Recall that this is a case in which the accused, as well as some of his codefendants and supporters, denied his culpability in the disappearance of Hellen Hanks. There were sharply conflicting accounts of many details, both before and during the January 1982 trial.

I have also made extensive use of quotations, with the various hearing and trial transcripts and newspaper and magazine articles being the prime sources. Since the transcript quotes were recorded by a court reporter directly as spoken, the syntax and phraseology oftentimes represent less-than-perfect English diction. On occasion, I have made minor corrections in the spelling and punctuation but generally reproduced quotes as written. Most of the time, the origin of a given quotation will be obvious, for example, dialogue from a hearing or the trial, or quotes from a legal ruling. In cases where the sources of quotations are not so clear, for example, most quotes from the media, I have documented these with endnotes in a Sources and References section at the end of the narrative. As is my custom, I have made liberal use of footnotes for the purpose of explanation or commentary.

In order to assist the reader in following this oftentimes-convoluted tale, I have supplied an appendix with two lists. The first is a timeline that lists the dates of major events in chronological order. The second is a listing of some of the individuals who played an important role in a saga which spans nearly half a century, together with a brief note as to what role they played. This list does not include every individual named in the book, but rather those whose actions, position, or testimony were important to the legal proceedings or understanding of the case.

So often in tales of true crime such as this, we focus on the crime itself, the accused, members of law enforcement, the investigation, and/or the attorneys who prosecute or defend their side of the case. While understandable, I urge the reader to recall the one silent voice in this story, that of the victim, Hellen Hanks. She was, by all accounts, an intelligent, honest, hard-working lady whose mission in life was to make the world better for her children and family. Her untimely death, by vile means and for evil purpose, should never be forgotten, nor should the sorrow suffered by her children and family.

William Rawlings
Sandersville, Georgia
September 1, 2019

Six Inches Deeper

The Disappearance of Hellen Hanks

Prologue

Six Inches Deeper

The light rain that began before midnight continued through the early morning hours, ushering in the soggy and overcast dawn of November 24, 1980. It had been a wet month, more so than usual, a minor hinderance for Fred Blanton, the logger who had purchased the 490-acre tract just south of Valdosta, Georgia, a year earlier. The property had belonged to Mildred Cothron, an inheritance after her husband's death in 1972. It had been on the market for a year and a half, and despite its close proximity to town and fifty acres of planted pine timber, no buyers had emerged. By late 1979 the asking price had dropped to what Blanton considered a reasonable bargain: $264,000, with seller financing after a $75,000 down payment.

Rather than keep the property as a timber tract, Blanton had other plans. With fertile soil and the mild climate of south Georgia, it would make for good cropland. He had clear-cut the standing timber on 300 acres, bulldozed up the stumps and burned them, and was in the final preparation stage of removing the remaining roots to make the land ready for plowing. By early afternoon of the 24th, the rain had stopped, allowing work to proceed. Fred was inspecting the progress of the job while his brother, Sidney Blanton, operated a Case tractor pulling a four-pronged chisel plow designed to cut into the soil and extract the roots. Fred had just driven up when his brother waved him over to show Fred what he had snagged with the plow's prongs.

Fred peered into the hole that had opened up just behind the plow. There was a box, appearing to be constructed of three-quarter-inch plywood covered with sheet metal. It measured roughly two feet by four feet in size and appeared to be about two feet deep. Fred said,

"Well, we got to get it up and out of the field because we can't plow over it."[1] They decided to try to pull it out of the ground by catching it with the plow. As Fred described it, "We taken that [chisel] plow and kept dropping it in, trying to pull it up, and every time we'd catch it, it'd tear a chunk off. And finally, I jumped in the hole, in the box and I told [my brother] to back up there and drop it down one more time and I'd see if I couldn't make it catch. And when I did, another fellow walked up and he said, 'You going to be found some bones in that box, you reckon?' And I picked up a bone and bumped it on the plow and he said, 'That looks like a leg bone to me.' And when he said that I dropped it and got out of the hole. And then we recognized what it was."

The top of the box had been eight or nine inches beneath the surface of the earth according to Fred Blanton's estimate. Later, when testifying in court, he was asked, "So if it had been maybe six inches deeper it'd still be there?"

"We'd never have found it," Blanton replied.

Chapter 1

There Are No Strangers in Valdosta[a]

From the perspective of the airliners that ply the routes between the resorts of Florida and the flight hubs of the upper Midwest, the city of Valdosta, Georgia, appears as a small island of urbanity set amidst a vast patchwork sea of green, a refuge of civilization surrounded by forests and fields. A few miles to the east, roads disappear into plantations of pine timber which themselves stop abruptly at the edge of the Great Okefenokee Swamp. To the west and north, areas more suited to human habitation, small villages appear every few miles, connected by long stretches of lonely two-lane highway. The Florida state line lies some fifteen miles to the south, but the Sunshine State's terrain, underlain by a deep shelf of limestone, laps up against Valdosta's southern limits. Here the land is completely flat, punctuated by seemingly innumerable sinkholes of various geologic age. Some have become peat-bog swamps, while others appear as rounded lakes known locally as "ponds."

Valdosta was created as a new settlement in 1860, its location chosen for its proximity to a rail line being constructed across the southern part of the state. The city's name was derived from Val d'Aosta, a country estate once owned by the governor who signed the act incorporating Lowndes County, of which Valdosta is the county seat. Over the ensuing decades, Valdosta became a regional center for commerce, its prosperity fueled by timber and turpentine as well as Sea Island cotton and other agriculture. The nascent city produced its share of prominent men; the famed dentist-turned-gambler-and-gunman John

---

[a] The title of this chapter is taken from the Valdosta/Lowndes County Chamber of Commerce slogan for 1971.

Henry "Doc" Holliday spent several of his teenage years here. Its fading fortunes in the twentieth century were revived by the opening of Interstate 75 in the mid-1960s. By the 1970s, as other rural areas were in decline, Lowndes County's population was growing rapidly. For most of its existence Valdosta was the sort of place where a man with an entrepreneurial spirit and the drive to see it through could become wealthy. One such man was "Foxy" Wilcox.

Ernest Keller Wilcox Sr. was born in Valdosta in 1907, the son of a widely respected local attorney.[2] In his early adolescence he was branded with the nickname of "Foxy," by which he would be informally known for the remainder of his life. His father, Elisha Kella Wilcox, had moved to Valdosta in 1900, three years after being admitted to the bar at age nineteen. By 1908 he had become one of the city's more prominent citizens, earning a listing in Valdosta's *Social Register*. Over the next two decades, prior to his unexpected death in 1938, the elder Wilcox was involved in a number of high-profile criminal and civil cases, including arguing a controversial case before the United States Supreme Court.

Like his father and older brother, Foxy chose the law as a profession, attending the University of Alabama School of Law and earning admission to the Georgia bar in 1932.[3] In 1945, at age thirty-eight, he married thirty-year-old Russell Plowden, one of the heirs to the Plowden fortune. It was the first marriage for both. Some six years later, in January 1951, the couple welcomed a son, Keller Wilcox Jr. He would be their only child.

With ambition, but perhaps not for the law, Foxy drifted into other areas of interest. By 1948, he had abandoned the law completely. That year he purchased the Lewis Outdoor Advertising Company, where he was employed as a manager. The business had originally been chartered in 1926 primarily for the purpose of erecting billboards along the state's growing highway system. The company was soon renamed Wilcox Outdoor Advertising. By all accounts, Foxy had finally found his niche in life. He was a natural salesman, a hail-fellow-well-met, an organizer and a planner. Foxy embraced his new profession, serving for more than two decades as an officer in the Georgia Outdoor Advertising Association. A listing of his greatest achievements included his earning "everlasting fame and the undying gratitude of the entire Outdoor Advertising Industry nationwide for his role in standing resolutely in the path of President Lyndon B. Johnson and Lady Bird Johnson and their determination to eliminate Outdoor as a national advertising medium."[4] "Lady Bird wanted the highways clear of billboards and junkyards, and filled with green landscaping and wildflowers." "Ugliness is so grim," she was quoted as saying.[5] Foxy Wilcox felt otherwise.

Under his ownership, the company grew steadily; by the early 1970s it had active accounts in more than fifty markets across south Georgia and north Florida. The growing business naturally required more space. In the spring of 1960 Wilcox Outdoor Advertising moved into a newly built office and warehouse located at 701 West Hill Avenue in Valdosta.

As their fortunes increased, the Wilcoxes also moved several times through a series of increasingly finer homes. In Valdosta, like many cities, wealth and social standing is often reflected in one's residence. The community is roughly divided by the main east-west rail line that slices through its downtown. South of the tracks the homes are modest, the businesses industrial, and the population largely African American. To the north of the city's historic center, the homes become grander and the population increasingly white. The exclusive Valdosta Country Club lies near the city's northern limits. By 1967 Foxy and Russell Wilcox were living in an architect-designed, newly constructed brick home located on Millpond Road, just a few hundred feet east of the southern end of Country Club Drive.

Whatever the fortunes of his parents, their son, Keller, was destined to achieve even greater fame, albeit under very different circumstances. As the only child of older parents, he apparently had an unremarkable childhood until the eighth grade, when they elected to send him to a residential military school, Admiral Farragut Academy in St.

Petersburg, Florida. The simple reason, his father later explained, was "he wasn't learning anything in the public schools." Keller attended Farragut for five years, graduating in 1969. All in all, his tenure there was unremarkable. He participated in intramural sports and was a member of the yearbook staff. The then-dean of students at Farragut would later describe him as "a model student."[6] Keller's senior yearbook write-up indicated he was planning to attend Valdosta State College. His future plans were otherwise unstated, though when "Farragut's 1969 seniors were asked to name their idols, Keller listed Hugh Hefner, the publisher of *Playboy* magazine."[7]

After graduation, Keller moved back to his parents' home on Millpond Road. He entered Valdosta State in 1969, initially wanting to pursue a career in medicine. He appears to have been a desultory student, soon switching his major to Business Administration before dropping out completely in the midst of his third year. With no clear direction in his life, and with a successful family business managed by an aging father, in the spring of 1972 Keller acceded to the obvious path and became a full-time employee of Wilcox Outdoor Advertising.

All considered, it was a positive move. The business was profitable and destined to be Keller's legacy from his parents. In fact, he already owned the land on which it was located, placed in trust for him at age nine, with full ownership due at age twenty-five. Merely maintaining the status quo would assure him a comfortable future.

And other things were going in Keller's favor as well. He was engaged to Jean King, with a wedding scheduled for early August 1972. A year younger than Keller, she was a lovely, long-haired brunette and fellow student at Valdosta State College. The two had met in the spring of 1970. She planned to finish her degree while Keller worked for the family business. There were social differences to be sure. Jean's father was a mechanic employed part time by Wilcox Advertising, but none of this seemed to matter. They appeared to be in love.

Following a series of pre-wedding parties, the young couple was married on Sunday, August 6th, at Valdosta's prestigious First Baptist

Church. They exchanged vows before an altar adorned with colorful arrays of flowers. Foxy served as his son's best man, while the bride was given in marriage by her father, their employer-employee status momentarily forgotten. The future seemed bright, but unbeknownst to any at the time, dark clouds were lingering just beyond the horizon.

Chapter 2

She Just Disappeared

For the first two decades of Foxy's ownership, Wilcox Outdoor Advertising had been a lean but successful business. Day-to-day management was Foxy's primary job, with office assistance from a secretary and marketing handled by a salesman. Keller assumed the latter role upon starting there full time in the spring of 1972. The actual work of erecting the billboards, changing the signage, and general maintenance in the company's far-flung markets fell to a team of trained laborers, all of whom were African American; "all colored,"[8] in Foxy's words. Many were long-term employees, some of whom had worked there for decades. The secretarial position was held by Hellen Griffin Hanks, a pretty, thirty-four-year-old mother of three who came to work at Wilcox Advertising in late January 1972.

By the early 1970s, the outdoor advertising industry found itself under attack from those who considered billboards an eyesore. In addition to ever-increasing local and state regulation, the Highway Beautification Act of 1965 put an end to the unlimited erection of billboards along some 300,000 miles of federal highways, in the process dealing a severe economic blow to many smaller regional advertising companies. With the family business threatened by events seemingly beyond his control, and facing his sixty-fifth birthday, Foxy made the decision to seek outside support. It was possible, even probable, that his son Keller would grow into the role of manager, but at the time he was new to the industry and still quite inexperienced. Accordingly, on August 1, 1972, Wilcox Outdoor Advertising entered into a management agreement with Lamar Advertising Company of Baton Rouge, Louisiana.

The Lamar firm, like Wilcox Advertising, traced its roots to the 1920s, but by the 1970s had become a major player in the southeastern billboard market. While continuing its core business of outdoor advertising, it sought to diversify by offering management and accounting services to a number of smaller firms, including Wilcox. Foxy and Keller were scheduled to meet several Lamar executives in Atlanta on August 30th, the same day that two other employees from Wilcox's Albany, Georgia, branch office were due in Valdosta to instruct the firm's secretary, Hellen Hanks, on a new computer-based bookkeeping system.

On Tuesday, August 29th, Keller and Foxy left Valdosta in Foxy's green 1970 Lincoln Continental, driving first to Albany to check on the branch office there, then proceeding on to Atlanta via Interstate 75. They arrived well after dark and checked into the Riviera Hyatt House Hotel at the junction of I-75 and Peachtree Road. The next afternoon they met with the president and executive vice president of Lamar Advertising, later that night going out for drinks and dinner in Underground Atlanta before returning to the hotel. The following morning the Wilcoxes headed back to Valdosta, on the way dropping off one of the Lamar executives at the Atlanta airport about 10:45 A.M. Keller drove, and on a whim, decided to stop in Cordele on the way back to visit briefly with Willard King, his father-in-law of just over three weeks. After about an hour, they were back on the interstate, arriving in Valdosta around 4:00 P.M. or soon after, according to statements given later. The two stopped long enough to pick up Keller's car, after which they drove separately to the Wilcox Advertising office, arriving (again, according to their estimates) around 4:30 P.M.

To their surprise, the office was empty. The front door was unlocked, the lights were all on, and a radio was playing softly in the background. Hellen Hanks was nowhere to be seen. Her car was parked in its usual spot with the keys in the ignition. Thinking she might be in the restroom, they waited a few minutes, then knocked on the door before opening it and finding it empty. A quick search of the premises revealed nothing. Keller walked over to the convenience store next door to inquire if anyone there had seen Hellen. No one had.

Thinking that there might have been an emergency, he called the local hospital, only to be told there was no record of her being seen there.

Shortly before 5:00 P.M., Keller called James Hanks, Hellen's husband, asking if she was at home. Hanks worked as a prison guard at the Lowndes Correctional Institution. At the time, he had been home about half an hour after completing his day shift. His wife's workday normally ended at five, so he was not aware of anything unusual. On being told that she was missing from work and could not be located, he asked Keller to notify the police and immediately left his home in Brooks County, arriving at Wilcox Advertising at approximately 5:25 P.M. The only one in the office at the time was Keller Wilcox, who was sitting at Hellen's desk, going through her pocketbook. Hanks asked him what he was doing, and Keller responded that he was "looking for some keys." He gave the pocketbook to Hanks, who found a set of keys he didn't recognize. He handed them back to Keller, who commented, "She won't be needing these anymore." Hanks took the pocketbook home.[9]

Two Valdosta policemen arrived shortly thereafter, soon followed by a third, who had heard the call on the radio. Both James Hanks and the police made a somewhat brief search of the building and the grounds. Nothing was found to indicate Hellen Hanks's whereabouts. There was no evidence of a struggle or signs of any violence. James Hanks left first, around 6:00 P.M., followed by the policemen, who left around 6:30 P.M. When questioned later, none of them reported seeing either Foxy Wilcox or his green Lincoln Continental; only Keller, and no one else. The incident was duly recorded as a missing persons case.[10] But the pocketbook Hellen Hanks left behind contained, in addition to her identification and photos of her children, applications for employment elsewhere. Both stated that she'd be available for employment on October 1, 1972, a month hence. She was planning to quit her job at Wilcox Outdoor Advertising.

Despite whatever disruption the disappearance of their secretary may have caused, Foxy and Keller had other plans for that evening.

Keller and his bride were the guests of honor at a dinner given for the newlyweds at Ocean Pond, some dozen or so miles south of Valdosta near the Florida state line. Naturally, the groom's father was expected, as were other members of the Wilcox family. More exclusive even than the Valdosta Country Club, the Ocean Pond Fishing Club[a] was originally founded in 1904 as a hunting and fishing preserve on an 880-acre sinkhole-lake of the same name. Activities revolved around a large, rambling, two-story wood-frame clubhouse dating from 1909. Both rustic and exclusive, it was the quintessential Southern "fish camp." The party was hosted by Dr. and Mrs. G. J. Austin, Keller's godparents, and Mr. and Mrs. Lamar Wansley, the local manager of the Georgia Power office where Jean, Keller's wife, worked while attending college. The party was due to start at 7:00 P.M.: cocktails first, then a seated dinner.

Around 5:00 P.M., Keller called his wife and instructed her to go on to the party by herself; he'd come later. Separately, Foxy called Dr. Austin and said he'd be running late. Both arrived at the Ocean Pond clubhouse around the same time, estimated to be approximately 9:00 P.M. by those who remembered. The guest list was small, fewer than twenty-five, and the initial absence and subsequent late arrival of the recent groom and his father was noted by all. Foxy and Keller were immediately surrounded by curious guests who wanted to know what had happened. For the first few minutes or so, Keller spoke with the guests, not acknowledging the presence of Jean, his new wife. She thought that somewhat odd. They'd only been married a bit more than three weeks. She had not seen him in more than two and a half days. After about fifteen or twenty minutes she went over and embraced him. As it was late, dinner was served in short order. Keller and Jean sat together as if nothing had happened. The evening was otherwise unremarkable.

---

[a] Originally incorporated as the Ocean Pond Hunting & Fishing Club. The current name dates from 1917.

The party broke up around 10:30 P.M. Keller told Jean that he needed to go back to the office to "make sure that everything was locked up."[11] She went home alone, going to bed about 11:00 P.M. She'd not heard from Keller by the time she drifted off to sleep but awoke the next morning to find him in bed. She had no idea what time he returned.

Chapter 3

Another Missing Person

To those who knew her, Hellen Griffin Hanks was not the sort of person to simply disappear. She was an intelligent, hard-working mother of three, apparently happily married for nearly sixteen years, a member of the Order of the Eastern Star, and active in the First Baptist Church in her home town of Morven, Georgia, some sixteen or so miles distant from Wilcox Outdoor Advertising. The only daughter among five children born to Turner and Mattie Griffin, she still lived in rural Brooks County, near where she was born. Hellen's great-grandfather settled there in the late 1860s after his service in the Confederate army.[12] Like their ancestors before them, Hellen's parents eked out a living from the earth, raising cotton, corn, and tobacco, with the whole family pitching in as needed to help plant and harvest the crops. A tall, slim girl of five feet, nine inches in height, Hellen excelled in academics and in sports, especially basketball.

In 1956 at age eighteen, a year after her graduation from high school, Hellen married James Harold Hanks, who during most of their marriage was employed in various law enforcement positions. Money was tight, and in addition to being the mother of three young children, she worked full time at secretarial and clerical jobs, attending to her family while pursuing continuing education courses at the local vocational school and college. Prior to going to work for the Wilcoxes, Hellen had been employed for ten years as a secretary-bookkeeper for the Langdale Company, a large local lumber mill. In early 1972, she was lured away by Foxy Wilcox with the offer of $120 a week, a twenty percent increase in her salary. On the job applications found in her pocketbook after she vanished, Hellen listed her concern that Wilcox Advertising was being "leased out," expressing fear that the Lamar

Company might not keep the office open. But there were other concerns as well, as later events would reveal.

As of the morning of September 1, 1972, the disappearance of Hellen Hanks was being treated as a missing persons case. It was at the Valdosta Police Department's morning report that day that Loyce Arnold, then assistant chief of police, first heard about the case. Arnold also served as the department's investigative officer, and in that capacity paid a visit to the Wilcox Advertising office later in the morning. Foxy and Keller were both there; neither reported any new information on Hellen Hanks or her whereabouts. The Wilcoxes were cooperative and recounted the events of the afternoon before. Arnold made a perfunctory search of the building and grounds, in addition to looking about the Union Oil Company building and the Minit Food Shop convenience store next door. Nothing was found.

Arnold spent the next several days investigating the case. Some interesting information was provided by a couple sitting on the front porch of 610 West Hill Avenue, almost exactly across the street. They reported that on the morning of August 31st they observed Hellen Hanks getting into an automobile with a white male, described as being of "short medium build, five-foot eight, probably around a hundred and sixty pounds" and having short, light-colored hair.[13] According to their observations, Mrs. Hanks, whom they recognized, appeared to be carrying something under her arm as she got into the car. The vehicle was described as either a Skylark or Cutlass—they disagreed on this—but were certain that it had a light blue bottom with a dark blue or black vinyl top, with an Alabama license plate.[14]

Foxy Wilcox went over the timeline of his and Keller's business trip to Atlanta. Although not mentioned initially, he did discover that two metal cash boxes were missing, one containing receipts and the other $52.40 in cash. Two Wilcox employees were interviewed, one of whom, Jerry Davis, was apparently the last person known to have seen Hellen Hanks on the morning of August 31st. According to a report Arnold dictated to a police department secretary, Davis stated that "he had seen Keller Wilcox pat Mrs. Hanks on the posterior region and that she had slapped him." Davis also reported that he'd overheard Keller "talking on the phone to someone and he used bad words in referring to Mrs. Hanks." His story was confirmed by another employee, John Goodman.[15]

On the possibility that marital problems or an extramarital affair may have led to Hellen's disappearance, Arnold individually interviewed her husband, James Hanks, her children, Lucy and David, as well as several members of the community who were acquainted with the family. Hellen's dissatisfaction with her job was confirmed, but there was no clear evidence that unhappiness at home or a secret relationship would cause her to leave. Expressing his opinion, Arnold reported, "I think now that she has probably got filled up with [James] Hanks and her job both so she has just left town for a while."[16]

The *Valdosta Daily Times* broke the news of Mrs. Hanks's disappearance on September 2nd in a front-page story under the headline, "Auto Said Linked to Missing Woman." With a smiling photo captioned, "Helen [*sic*] Hanks, Mother of Three," the account went on to say that two cash boxes had also been discovered to be missing, one of which supposedly contained "around $200." Assistant Chief Arnold told the paper that the "possibilities were she either ran away or was kidnapped but he has information to discount both theories." The nature of the information was not revealed.

A week passed without a break in the case. It came to light that Hellen had a scheduled appointment with her hairdresser on August 31st after work but had not cancelled and didn't show up. She had put her typewriter in her car planning to take it to the repair shop, but it was still there when she vanished. There were no phone calls to family or friends. The September 7th edition of the *Times* reported the absence of new leads under the headline, "Search Has Gotten Nowhere," despite a $1,000 reward offered by "relatives and friends" of Hellen Hanks. Photographs of the missing woman had been sent to area police departments and broadcast on television stations in Albany, Thomasville, Atlanta, and Columbus.

The one seemingly positive lead turned out to be useless. The man allegedly observed with Hellen Hanks on August 31st was someone from Wilcox's Albany office working on the new computer-based bookkeeping system. What the couple had described was partially accurate; the man's vehicle did indeed have an Alabama tag. But his visit had taken place on Wednesday, August 30th, the day before Mrs. Hanks's disappearance. The missing cash boxes, however, remained a puzzle.

It was Keller Wilcox's new father-in-law who discovered what would become an important clue. Willard King was a full-time employee of the Pepsi-Cola Bottling Company in Cordele, but he worked part time on weekends for Wilcox Advertising. His primary job was maintenance work on the small fleet of Wilcox vehicles, mainly work trucks used to erect and maintain the company's billboards.

On Saturday, September 9th, King reported for work as usual at the West Hill Avenue office and warehouse. Keller Wilcox was at home with his wife. King backed his work truck into the warehouse, following his usual habit of taking his toolbox off the back of his truck in order to place it on top of a spare poster box located near his workspace. The heavy tool kit, weighing between 250 and 300 pounds, was easier to reach when it was on top of a box a couple of feet off the concrete floor. To his annoyance, the box which had always been in the same spot in the warehouse was not there. King called Keller, who apparently had not missed the box, one of three similar containers the company had in use at the time. They discussed it, deciding that since Hellen Hanks and the box had disappeared about the same time, the police should be notified. Keller made the call. Assistant Chief Arnold responded by coming back to the warehouse to inspect things for himself. After a few minutes' conversation, Arnold dismissed the significance of the missing box and its possible connection to the missing woman, stating, "She didn't leave here in a box, she left here with a man."[17] He did not bother to make a report of the incident.

Hellen Hanks's disappearance remained a missing persons case. It was not to be the only one during the long summer of 1972. In mid-June, a teenager from Lowndes County and her friend who had recently moved to Miami from Valdosta went missing. Their car was found several weeks later in Ocala, Florida, but it was early August before they were reported safe in Jacksonville, Florida, apparently having run away. On September 11th, another Morven, Georgia, resident, forty-six-year-old Elva Lee Jones, disappeared. Her abandoned car was found the next day in Dade City, Florida.[a]

In the Valdosta of the early 1970s, there was the perception of a significant increase in major crime. The use of illegal drugs, notably marijuana, was on the rise, especially among students at Valdosta State College. The Valdosta Police Department ran a large undercover operation, resulting in a number of students being charged with felony drug possession. There were several high-profile murder cases as well, including the death of sixty-eight-year-old Grady Massey, a cotton buyer for the Strickland Cotton Mill. He was found dead in his office by a secretary and an office machine repairman who had heard him cry out moments before. Massey was examined on the scene by the county coroner and a doctor before the body was carried to the hospital where he was formally pronounced dead due to natural causes, allegedly a "massive internal hemorrhage." It was only several hours later that workers at the local funeral home discovered that Massey had died of a stab wound to his chest, apparently during a robbery attempt.[18] Relatively speaking, a simple missing persons case had become a lower priority for local law enforcement.

The perceived crime wave was not limited to Valdosta or Lowndes County. On October 3rd, less than five weeks after Hellen Hanks

---

[a] More than a year and a half later, an escaped convict and serial killer confessed to strangling Evans and hiding the body.

vanished, Judge George Horkan of the five-county Southern Judicial Circuit appealed to Governor Jimmy Carter to send in additional investigators to "help local police agencies clear up numerous missing persons and hit-and-run reports."[19] Within days, Governor Carter responded by sending Ronald Angel, the state's "top criminal investigator" and agent-in-charge of the Georgia Bureau of Investigation's Major Crime Squad. Citing a September "mysterious" double murder in Thomas County, three women in the district who were "missing without a trace," three hit-and-run deaths, plus three other unsolved murders, the governor sought to quell the concerns of local citizens who had "become apprehensive about their safety."[20] Angel's top priority was an inquiry into the fate of Hellen Hanks.

In recognition of the fact that Mrs. Hanks had been missing for more than a month with no attempt to contact her friends or family, foul play was considered a major possibility. Agents interviewed her immediate "family, relatives, associates and people in nearby working places."[21] Her husband, James Hanks, was immediately excluded as a suspect. In his job as a prison guard at the Lowndes Correctional Institution, he'd been locked inside at the time of her disappearance.

On October 11th, Senior Agent Ronald Angel, accompanied by Agents D. J. Delancey and Larry Oxford, interviewed Keller Wilcox. The meeting took place in one of the rooms at Valdosta's Holiday Inn near I-75. One of the agents' primary concerns was the establishment of Keller's whereabouts at the time of his secretary's disappearance. Keller was cooperative, speaking freely and without hesitation. Once again, he gave the details of his and his father's business trip to Albany and Atlanta, stating that they arrived back in Valdosta about 3:45 P.M. on August 31st, and at the Wilcox Advertising office about fifteen minutes later. The agents were later able to corroborate his account by obtaining receipts from their hotel in Atlanta and contacting individuals whom they met while there. In response to "some alleged incidents" gleaned from their conversations with Hellen's family and others, Keller denied to the agents that he'd ever called her "a whore or a bitch over the telephone" or to her face. He denied that he had "ever patted or touched her" or that "she had ever slapped him."[22]

After three or four weeks of investigation in south Georgia, no clear leads as to the fate of Hellen Hanks had been established. The trail went cold, its details and reports filed with other unsolved missing persons cases.

Chapter 4

The Other Victims

The sun was low in the western sky when James Hanks returned to his modest brick home in Morven on the evening of August 31st. As he would remark years later, "She might leave me, but she'd never have left the children."[23] Earlier, he had picked up fifteen-year-old Lucy, who had been at her high school art teacher's house. David, age thirteen, and Penny, a ten-year-old fifth grader, waited nervously in the yard, uncertain as to what had happened to their mother. Inside, their granny was on the phone with their uncle Steve. Hanks seemed both nervous and confused as he stepped out of his white F-150 pickup. When asked what had occurred, he replied, "I'm not sure. Wilcox said she was gone when they got back from Atlanta this afternoon."

It was a problem for adults, and the grown-ups tried earnestly at first to shield the children from the desperately worrisome truth. The following afternoon, David recalled returning home after school to find about forty cars and trucks in their driveway and along the dirt road leading to the house. Promises were made by friends and family and assurances of help given for the future, whatever the outcome might be. A day passed, and then the next without word from their mother. James Hanks felt overwhelmed. Penny had never seen her father cry before, but recalled him sobbing, sitting on the living room sofa that none of the children were allowed to use.

Days turned into weeks. The possibility dawned that perhaps Hellen might never be coming back. One afternoon James Hanks sat down with Lucy, David, and Penny and shared with them the stark reality of the situation; their mother was gone, and it was up to them to take care of things. Money was tight, he confirmed, and they would all have to pull together to make things work. Among the items found in Hellen's pocketbook was her savings account register from the Citizens Bank of

Morven. The balance was $193.13, with the last deposit made more than six months before she vanished.

Over the coming months, Lucy, barely on the cusp of adulthood, assumed by default the role of "lady of the house," taking charge of the day-to-day running of the household. David and Penny each dealt with their mother's absence in their own way. Penny, based on what she'd seen in television mysteries, imagined that her mother had been kidnapped and in the process of fighting her abductor was hit over the head, causing her to lose her memory. Just like in the movies and on TV, all it would take was another blow to the head and her memories would come pouring back. She'd come home to her family. But she did not.

Privately, each of the children tried to understand why their mother left. Were they somehow responsible, or could it have been something at her work or elsewhere that they didn't know about or understand? Thinking back, Penny recalled snatches of a conversation between her parents about something that had happened on the job. "I'll go down there and straighten him out," her father said angrily, to which her mother replied, "No, James, you can't do that."[24] Years later she would realize the meaning of these strange words.

As summer became fall and the investigation of Hellen Hanks's disappearance produced no leads, news stories and public interest gradually turned elsewhere. Penny, still ten years old in December 1972, recalled a particularly bountiful Christmas, realizing only years later that it was paid for by money donated to the Hankses by friends and family.

As if the uncertainty of their mother's absence were not enough, the rumors and taunts at school made life for Lucy, David, and Penny all the more painful. Hellen Hanks had chosen to abandon her family and run off with another man, or so they said. A boy at school told Penny, "I know where your mama is." There were reports that she had been sighted in Florida, New York, Bermuda, and elsewhere. Later, when Penny was old enough to drive, she saw a lady in Quitman "who looked just like Mama and moved like her. I followed her into a store and then she turned around."[25] Another faint hope was dashed.

One of the biggest blows to family unity came in early to mid-1973, when the children awoke to find that their father had brought home a woman the night before. Lucy screamed at the top of her lungs, accusing him of betraying her mother. She wanted this woman out of the house.[26] Within months, the woman, an "old girlfriend" from James Hanks's high school years, had moved in, together with her teenage son. Lucy, now older, moved out to live with a friend's family in Valdosta, finding a job at a convenience store near the interstate to provide her with some income. David, the same age as the woman's son, became passive-aggressive. Penny worried about what would happen if Mama came home and found this woman in her house. Without telling his children, James Hanks quietly began divorce proceedings against his missing wife in the spring of 1974. The final decree was filed on September 30, 1974.

While the memory of Hellen Hanks faded from public consciousness, the Hanks family, wounded by her loss, struggled on. With her absence, the dream of college for the children faded as well; there was no money to pay for it. Even before Hellen's disappearance, the children had worked during the summer to earn money. After she was gone this became a necessity. By that time, Lucy had a "real" job, but David and Penny toiled summers on their great-uncle Jack's farm, harvesting tobacco in the sweltering south Georgia heat. The workdays were long, from 7:00 A.M. to 7:00 P.M., cropping, handling, stringing, and stocking the tobacco leaves. There were breaks, of course, and a generous lunch, but the labor was hard, dirty, and for the Hanks children, necessary. Their uncle paid them generously, enough to buy their own school supplies.

Even with time and the complete lack of news about their missing mother, the mystery of her disappearance continued. Lucy, as the oldest, was called by Keller Wilcox on several occasions, asking, "How's your mama?" He alleged that the family, and Lucy in particular, knew her whereabouts.[27] In the mid-1970s a dispatcher for the Valdosta Police Department received a call from a woman who claimed that she was Hellen Hanks. She wanted to assure the dispatcher that she was alive and well, living in Texas, and wanted her kids to know that she loved them.[28] In an unrelated incident around the same time, Lucy was contacted at work by someone from the Valdosta police, who told her, "We have reason to believe that you've been in contact with your mother."[29] As events would later make clear, these allegations and threads of hope were no more than fantasy.

Lucy, the oldest, married a few years out of high school. The marriage collapsed after about a year. David, the middle child, wanted to be an engineer. He was accepted for admission to Georgia Tech in Atlanta, taking a summer job on the railroad driving spikes and lifting crossties to earn money, but it was not enough. At his father's urging, he joined the Navy.[a] Penny, the youngest, was more fortunate. A woman she scarcely knew, aware of the family's tragedy and Penny's academic record, offered her a full scholarship to Georgia Southwestern College, paying for her tuition, housing, and meals.

Time passed. The fall of 1979 would have marked seven years since their mother's disappearance. Despite the rumors and alleged sightings, there was no evidence at all that Hellen Hanks was still alive. Hoping to help heal the wounds of her loss, Lucy believed that a memorial service and the erection of a monument would be an appropriate way to acknowledge the obvious and perhaps help Hellen's family

---

[a] Despite his initial educational disappointment, David Hanks went on to a successful career. On joining the Navy, he entered the Nuclear Power Program and served on the nuclear-powered aircraft carrier the USS Nimitz. Following his discharge, he earned a degree in nuclear engineering and was appointed an international nuclear safeguards inspector by the International Atomic Energy Agency (IAEA) in 2002. In 2005, his efforts and those of others resulted in the IAEA receiving the Nobel Peace Prize for its "efforts to prevent nuclear energy from being used for military purposes and to ensure that nuclear energy for peaceful purposes is used in the safest possible way."

and friends achieve some closure. She asked her brother David, now stationed aboard the USS Nimitz, to search for an appropriate inscription. In response, he tried to imagine what his mother might say to her grandchildren one day, should she ever meet them. Words from Bob Dylan's "Forever Young" came to mind: *May you be courageous, stand up right, and be strong.*

In the fall of 1979, friends and family gathered for a ceremony held in the Campground Cemetery near the family church in Morven. Over an empty grave, a simple marble monument was dedicated to the "Hopes and Dreams of Hellen Griffin Hanks." This was to be the end. Hellen's husband, James, chose not to attend. He would remarry a few months later. David Hanks, on leave from the military, recalled finding some measure of closure and a small bit of peace with the ceremony. All this would be shattered on November 24, 1980.

Chapter 5

Three Thousand and Seven Days

Viewed from nearly half a century later, the world of the 1970s seems almost archaic, a distant and sometimes discredited time of change. The generation of the '60s was coming of age and beginning to assume roles of leadership and influence in the world of their parents. The Old South, the rural agrarian society of the post-Civil War era, was changing, often in ways that seemed threatening to the status quo. 1972 saw Richard Nixon's groundbreaking visit to Communist China, the invention of the CT scan,[a] the introduction of email, and the death of J. Edgar Hoover. Shoichi Yokoi, a World War II Japanese soldier who had hidden out in the jungles of Guam since 1945, was captured and reluctantly repatriated to his country, stating, "We Japanese soldiers were told to prefer death to the disgrace of getting captured alive." The FBI for the first time began hiring female agents, and the Watergate burglars were arrested, leading to President Nixon's resignation under threat of impeachment two years later.

In Georgia, the year 1972 was notable for the completion of the sculptures of Jefferson Davis, Robert E. Lee, and Stonewall Jackson on Stone Mountain's northern scarp, finishing a project that had begun in 1915 through the efforts of the United Daughters of the Confederacy and with the support of the Ku Klux Klan. In Brooks County, home to the Hanks family, the *Quitman Free Press* announced in a front-page headline, "Negro Woman Jailed on Murder Charge," as if her race might confirm her predilection to such criminal acts.[30] Around the same time, the *Press* reported that state and federal revenue agents

---

[a] Computerized Axial Tomography, commonly know as CT or CAT scanning.

had dynamited a local bootlegger's moonshine whiskey still[31] and that the telephone company hoped that "within the next two years" subscribers would be able to make long distance calls without having to go through an operator.[32]

Perhaps in response to the threat of change, a grand jury in Lowndes County began a local anti-smut campaign in the summer of 1973, issuing an order to "clean up pornography in the county." Shortly thereafter, authorities began confiscating copies of *Playboy*, *Penthouse*, and *Oui* magazines off local newsstand racks. When interviewed by the press about these actions, Assistant Police Chief Loyce Arnold stated, "The grand jury wanted this. It's not up to the Police Department to interpret this. It's up to the courts to say after we enforce it." Arnold also added that he believed books came under the same ruling. "The way I'm going to decide it is if I pick it up and it has obscene words in it, then I'm going to make a case against the distributor. It's up to him to worry about it then." "A major magazine distributor in the area labeled the police move as 'censorship,'" commenting that local supporters of the crackdown "don't even know what pornography is."[33]

While local grand juries might have aspired to improve the morals of the community, lingering questions remained about the honesty of the constabulary. Some conspiracy theorists had even speculated that members of law enforcement might have had some role in Hellen Hanks's disappearance, if not directly, then perhaps in covering up a crime. It could have been a reasonable conjecture; pornography aside, the police seemed to have turned a blind eye toward illegal and often lucrative enterprises. The existence of a local numbers racket, familiarly referred to as "The Bug," was widely known, as were slot machines and gambling in a number of private clubs. In July 1973, Jewell Futch, the sheriff of Lowndes County since 1949 and a charter member of the Georgia Sheriffs Association, was indicted by a federal grand jury on charges that he "took money to protect gambling" and obstructed the work of other law enforcement agencies.[34] The sheriff called the charges "politically motivated," explaining, "I took for granted it was what the people wanted."[35] Convicted later that year, Futch continued to serve as sheriff until April 1975 while his case was on appeal.[b] Separately, in August 1974, a local jury refused to convict him on a fifty-count indictment for "stealing county funds."[36] The jury accepted Futch's contention that he had used the funds to pay informants.

If the decade of the 1970s was one of tragedy and sadness for the Hanks family, it was in many ways the opposite for the Wilcoxes. The disappearance of Hellen Hanks seemed to have had no impact on Wilcox Advertising, a mere bump in the road which—on a practical basis—likely served to increase awareness of a thriving local business. With time, Keller Wilcox gradually took his place beside his father, taking on greater management responsibilities and eventually assuming the title of president. The son and heir of a wealthy and prominent family, he slipped easily into what many might assume was his preordained role in life. "Keller joined the Valdosta Chamber of Commerce, the North Valdosta Rotary Club, the Touchdown Club, and the local Boy's Club, which Foxy helped start. He was an ardent booster, a dedicated joiner, and likeable young man on the make—someone, as a longtime observer of Valdosta's social emergings remarked, 'with a future as shiny as a new silver dollar.'"[37] The one blemish on what seemed to be an assured future was the breakup of his first marriage.

Besides his other activities, Keller Wilcox took a keen interest in law enforcement. In the mid-1970s, he began serving as a volunteer auxiliary policeman.[c] This program, ostensibly designed to increase public interest and awareness of law enforcement's role in the community, allowed participants direct access to police headquarters,

---

[b] Then-ex-Sheriff Futch entered federal prison in October 1975. He died a few weeks later of heart disease.

[c] The year that Keller Wilcox became a member of the police auxiliary is somewhat uncertain. Keller testified at trial that he joined in 1977, but Herman Lyle, a retired FBI agent, testified that he was a member in 1974.

information about local crime, as well as the opportunity to wear a uniform and ride on patrol with local officers. It may have been through this activity that Keller met Neil Johannessen.

Johannessen was a handsome detective with the Valdosta Police Department. About five years older than Wilcox, he and his wife, Delia, became social friends with Keller and his wife, Jean. Apparently well respected in his profession, he was president of the local Fraternal Order of Police and, importantly, the National Crime Information Center officer in charge of liaison with the federally sponsored national intelligence network.[d] In this position he had access to information regarding confidential investigations, information not available to the police force at large. Keller would later describe him as "one of his best friends."[38] Somehow, Jean became involved with Neil.

On May 11, 1979, Jean Wilcox filed for divorce from Keller. Four days later, Delia Johannessen filed for divorce from her husband, Neil. Both divorces were finalized at the end of the required thirty-day waiting period, Jean's on June 12th and Delia's two days later. In November, a bit more than five months after her divorce decree, the former Mrs. Keller Wilcox became the new Mrs. Neil Johannessen. Ironically, the newly married Johannessens moved into the duplex at 2808 Walmar Place, the same home where Jean and Keller had begun their marriage some seven years earlier. Jean continued teaching school, while Neil continued his job as a police detective.

On Wednesday, March 12, 1980, Jean returned home from work at about 5:15 P.M. She was surprised to discover that all the doors to her residence were locked from the inside. The police were summoned and forcibly entered the house. Inside, they found Johannessen dead, his "partially clothed" body in a horizontal position with a tie-down

---

[d] National Crime Information Center (NCIC): The NCIC was created by the FBI under J. Edgar Hoover in 1967 for the purpose of coordinating crime-related information among and between local, state, and federal law enforcement agencies.

strap with hooks on each end wrapped around his neck and attached to a doorknob. Sheriff Robert Carter gave the presumed cause of death as "sexual asphyxiation." According to investigating officers, it appeared that Johannessen "was engaged in some form of sexual fetish or ritual and accidentally hanged himself." He had been married to his new wife for less than four months. The *Valdosta Daily Times* carried the story on its front page, citing "a criminal investigation textbook put out by the University of Georgia," while noting, "Some officers from the city and county forces have attended criminal investigation courses and said sexual asphyxiation is often confused with suicide."[39]

The *Times*'s reporting of Johannessen's death brought a barrage of negative comments castigating the paper for its "distasteful," "cruel," and "thoughtless" reporting. In letters to the editor, many defending the dead man's family, one reader called for a public apology, saying, "What Mr. Johannessen did in his personal life is his own business." Another suggested, "This type of reporting belongs in a second-rate gossip paper and is a disgrace to Valdosta." Rumors swirled as to other possible explanations for his death, but a detailed investigation by authorities appeared to confirm the original assumption of its cause.[40]

About a month prior to Neil Johannessen's death, Keller Wilcox had begun dating Sonia Patricia Lasseter, a local high school guidance counselor and daughter of a prominent and wealthy family from Moultrie, Georgia.[41] Sonia had been a contemporary of Keller's at Valdosta State College, but it is unclear if they knew each other during their student years. After a relatively brief six-month courtship, Sonia and Keller were married on October 25, 1980, in Moultrie's First Baptist Church. Those who attended described the wedding as an elegant affair. This time, Bob Bolton, a friend of Keller's, served as the groom's best man. The newlyweds settled back in Valdosta, perhaps looking forward to a lifetime of happiness. As the Fates would have it, however, the Blanton brothers would make their gristly discovery a month later on the dreary afternoon of November 24, 1980, and in the process changed the trajectory of multiple lives. Three thousand and seven days had passed since Hellen Hanks went missing.

Chapter 6

The Buried Box

The lead headline on the front page of the Tuesday, November 25, 1980, afternoon edition of the *Valdosta Daily Times* read, "Missing Valdosta Woman's Body Found," illustrated by two photos and accompanied by a four-column article. There was the same smiling headshot of Helen [*sic*] Hanks the paper had run at the time of her disappearance in 1972, plus another larger image of Dr. Jim Howard of the State Crime Laboratory, and Loyce Arnold, now Valdosta police chief. Both men were examining "the skull found Monday." The article briefly recounted the accidental discovery of the buried box at about 5:00 P.M. the preceding afternoon by the Blanton brothers, as well as Fred Blanton's "I went looking for me a sheriff" comment once he realized the box appeared to contain human bones. Less than twenty-four hours after the discovery, a "90 percent positive" identification had been made based on Hellen Hanks's dental records originally collected during the 1972 missing person investigation.

Early reports described the makeshift coffin as a "tin-reinforced plywood box, about four feet long, three feet wide, and two to three feet deep[a]...buried about 18 inches under the ground."[42] The sun had set by the time law enforcement personnel arrived at the burial site, located off a dirt road about six miles—a ten- to twelve-minute drive—from the Wilcox Advertising office and warehouse in Valdosta. The

---

[a] Various estimates were given of the box's size. An accurate description given at trial from one of the officers who helped recover evidence at the scene described it as being "approximately four-feet long and two-feet wide, and two-feet high built with three-quarter-inch marine plywood and covered with...galvanized sheet metal."

North Lowndes County Volunteer Fire Department brought in a portable generator and overhead lights. A team from the Southwestern Regional State Crime Lab in Moultrie, about forty miles away, was summoned for assistance as examination began of what was now a crime scene. For the next several hours and continuing into the following morning, officers from both the Lowndes County Sheriff's Department (LCSD) and the Valdosta police, assisted by personnel from the state crime lab, carefully excavated the buried box and surrounding earth. Sieves were used to screen the soil for fine bits of evidence.

The missing person case was now a homicide investigation. As the murder was presumed to have taken place within the city limits and the body was found in unincorporated Lowndes County, Chief Arnold and Lowndes Sheriff Robert Carter organized a joint city-county investigative team, headed by Captain Billy Register from the city and Detective Sergeant Billy Selph from the county.

Overnight "about 80 percent" of the victim's skeleton was recovered. Despite the relatively small size of the box, investigators initially reported that the body did not appear to have been dismembered. An assortment of other evidence was found in and around the ersatz casket. There was a C&S Bank bag, two metal petty-cash boxes, and a bundle of papers dating from 1972. Personal items included what appeared to be a green dress and a string of green beads, the clothing that Hellen Hanks was said to be wearing on the day of her disappearance. Also recovered were a princess ring, sandals, a single earring, panty hose, underwear, and a brassiere. Interestingly, the *Times* reported that the box in which the remains were found was "tentatively identified by an officer of Wilcox Advertising as one of a kind they at one time used on trucks to protect sign material from the weather."[43] This appeared to be the same box—or one similar to it—reported missing a bit more than a week after Hanks vanished eight years earlier. The "officer of Wilcox Advertising" was Keller Wilcox.

On Monday evening, about 7:00 P.M., Sonia Wilcox answered a phone call from a man who asked to speak to Keller. The caller identified himself as someone with the Lowndes County Sheriff's Department. As Keller would recount later, "He went into this story about finding a wooden box, a buried wooden box with a skeleton in it."[44] Keller initially thought this might be a hoax. "Over the years," he explained, "I had gotten numerous telephone calls or various policemen had told me...that Mrs. Hanks had been found." This time, he concluded, it might be true. He tried to reach Herman Lyle, a retired FBI agent with whom he'd earlier discussed the Hellen Hanks case. When he couldn't reach Lyle, he called Bob Bolton, the best man in his recent wedding. Bolton was able to find Lyle, and after an initial conversation, the three men rode over to the county jail to see what was going on.

At the jail, the deputies were awaiting Dr. Jim Howard from the crime lab. Shortly after his arrival, a caravan of cars set off for the burial site, arriving around 9 P.M. Bob Bolton rode with Dr. Howard, while Keller rode with Herman Lyle. Keller stayed about "an hour and a half or so" watching the group of law enforcement officers "dig stuff out of the hole" and screen the soil for evidence. He knew the majority of them, many from his involvement as a volunteer member of the police auxiliary. Before leaving, he confirmed to investigators that the newly unearthed box appeared similar to the one reported missing in 1972 from Wilcox Advertising.

David Hanks was at the naval base in Norfolk, Virginia, when he received word of the discovery of his mother's remains. He requested an emergency leave and drove home, going straight to his mother's memorial, the empty grave. Later he would recall "a sudden sadness I'd avoided for eight years. Her death was finally confirmed. Who was responsible was a distant second thought."[45]

Penny, who was in college at the time, hid her pain and the family secret of her mother's unknown fate by never speaking of the subject to her friends and classmates. She recalled,

> *Once, while I was telling a family story, someone in the group pointed out that I never talked about my mother, only my dad. It caught me off guard. I had never said the words "she is dead" so I couldn't say that*

in response. I think I mumbled something about her "not being around," which didn't sound that great either. But then one evening, as we were talking in one of our rooms, someone told me the phone in the hallway was for me. It was my stepmother telling me "they have found your mama's body." She told me Daddy said he couldn't tell me, but they wanted me to hear it from them before I heard it on the news. I was in shock, I think. I went back to my college friends and poured out the whole sordid story as I knew it, which really wasn't that much. I could only tell them that my mother had been missing for over eight years with not a trace and no clues. Now her remains were discovered and I didn't know how to process that. I was still only eighteen, and sheltered.[46]

The Wednesday, November 26th, edition of the *Times* revealed a few more facts about the evidence discovered at the burial site, and suggested that rapid progress was being made in the investigation. Hellen Hanks's remains had been taken to Moultrie for further examination by a state crime lab pathologist. It was assumed that she was killed near the time she went missing, leading authorities to focus on those who had been contemporaneous employees of Wilcox Advertising. The suspects had been narrowed to a list of "about 12." Chief Arnold announced that "lie detector tests are going to be given to all present and most former employees of the company, along with others." The article also provided more details about the evidence found at the burial site. The green dress that Hanks was wearing when she disappeared was found "in the ground beneath the box, indicating it had been removed." It "appeared to have been cut away from the body." A heavy lock and key were found near the dress. The underwear, also found outside of the makeshift coffin, was wadded up in a ball. Hellen Hanks was evidently nude when her body was placed in the box. Arnold said he was "working on the theory the death 'was a sex crime..., there are some rather unusual aspects to the case.'"

By Friday, November 28th, the number of suspects in Hellen Hanks's murder had been narrowed to "about half a dozen," according to Chief Arnold.[47] Investigators were said to be "working on the theory that the woman was killed by someone who at one time either worked with the company or had knowledge of its operations." Arnold went on to comment that there were several "good" suspects in the case. There would either be a quick arrest or a "long dry spell."

By Sunday, six days after the discovery of the body, no additional progress had been made.[48] The *Times*'s daily report from investigating officers was now more tentative. No new evidence had been discovered, and investigators were having some difficulty in locating a number of individuals they wanted to interview. James Hanks gave a statement praising Chief Arnold and strongly criticizing Wilbar Perkerson, the Valdosta police chief in 1972 at the time of his wife's disappearance. "He made a statement at the time that she probably went to Florida," Hanks said. "I'd like somebody to tell that s.o.b. that she didn't go there." Perkerson was said to be unavailable for comment.

On the ninth day after the discovery, detectives announced "a possible break in the case."[49] After an intensive search, only two of Wilcox Advertising's past employees had been found. The problem was the unavailability of old employment records, no longer maintained in Valdosta since the company's affiliation with Lamar Advertising. Records were expected to arrive in the mail any day from Lamar's offices in Baton Rouge. Investigators hoped these would be the source of new leads. Even with this glimmer of hope, progress in the investigation seemed to grind to a halt. Newspaper coverage and public announcements became infrequent as detectives worked quietly behind the scenes, keeping news of their interviews, evidence analysis, and other information to themselves.

The investigators were bombarded with tips, many of which found their roots in false rumors and innuendo. Through December and into the new year, dozens of potential witnesses were interviewed, including a number of past and then-current employees of the Wilcoxes. Within days of the discovery of Hellen Hanks's remains, members of the investigative task force contacted Wilcox Advertising, inquiring if there were other work boxes in the company's possession that could be compared to remains of the now-shattered box that had been used to bury the body. Willard King, with Keller's permission, found one in the junk pile behind the office, buried beneath some lumber. Officers dug it out and took it away as evidence. [50]

Throughout the spring of 1981, the investigation quietly continued. In mid-March, Captain Billy Register revealed to the local newspaper that a "witness" with potential information on the case had been located in Helen, Georgia.[51] This turned out to be another dead end. A few weeks later he reported that detectives were working "to solidify a case for an arrest."[52] Besides the encouraging news, he also noted that the task force was still awaiting the final report from the State Crime Lab in Atlanta on the evidence found at the gravesite. An exact cause of the victim's death had not yet been determined.

Even though both Foxy and Keller Wilcox seemed to have reliable alibis as to their whereabouts on the day Hellen Hanks disappeared, attention increasingly turned in their direction as other potential leads went cold. Based on interviews with the victim's family and friends, it was confirmed that Hellen had been unhappy in her job and was searching elsewhere for employment at the time of her disappearance. The job applications found in her pocketbook appeared to confirm this. There was talk of "sexual harassment."[b] Over the next few months investigators would make "numerous" visits to Wilcox Advertising, interviewing both father and son.[53]

In mid-June, Hellen Hanks's remains were returned to the family by the State Crime Lab. In spite of intensive efforts, the eight years spent resting in the lonely grave off Indian Ford Road and the damage inflicted by the chisel plow had obscured the details needed to establish a definitive cause of death. The Hanks family assembled once again at the memorial monument they had erected in the Campground

---

[b] The term "sexual harassment" is sometimes thought to be an early twenty-first century term but was in use in the early 1980s. In certain employment situations it is deemed a potential violation of the Civil Rights Act of 1964.

Cemetery more than a year earlier. With sadness, but with a sense of closure as to her fate, her remains were once again, and this time permanently, returned to the earth. Or so everyone believed at the time.

Chapter 7

A Phone Call at 3:30 A.M.

At 3:30 A.M. on the morning of Friday, July 3, 1981, the phone rang in Keller and Sonia Wilcox's bedroom at 2403 Riverside Drive in Valdosta.[54] Keller picked up the receiver, only to be greeted with silence. The couple had planned to spend the weekend at the family's condo at Fernandina Beach, Florida, a two-and-a-half-hour drive to the east. They had originally planned to leave the night before, but at the last minute decided to wait until the next day. Now awake, Keller lay in bed for a while, considering getting up and heading out early for the beach. He was about to suggest this to Sonia when the doorbell rang. It was now 4:30 A.M. Grabbing a pistol he kept at the bedside, Keller went to his back door, the entrance to his garage. Through the window, he could make out two male figures in the semidarkness. Initially thinking that it was his father and uncle who had come to tell him something had happened to his mother, he opened the door and recognized Sheriff Robert Carter and Police Chief Loyce Arnold. He invited them in and took his gun back to the bedroom.

The officers said they wanted Keller to come with them, explaining that they needed to talk with him. Keller replied, "Well, let me get a shower and I'll come down and meet y'all wherever y'all say." The men were insistent, not yet revealing the exact nature of why they were there at this odd hour of the morning. They asked if he wanted a lawyer, in response to which Keller reminded them that he'd spoken with them on a number of occasions without an attorney present. Why should he need one now? A warrant for his arrest had been issued, Carter replied. Sonia asked, "For what?" The reply was "Murder." They asked again, "Do you want a lawyer?" This time Keller replied, "Yes."

Keller called Wilby Coleman, a local attorney to whom he was related by marriage.[a] Coleman at first thought the early-morning call was a joke, but on realizing it was not, agreed to meet him at the county jail. A squad car was waiting outside of Keller's house to take him there.

For weeks rumors had circulated in Valdosta that Foxy and Keller Wilcox were now the prime suspects in the murder of Hellen Hanks. The word on the street held that their arrests were imminent. When Keller returned home from a business trip to Albany the evening before his arrest, Sonia told him of a rumor that he "had been arrested for the murder" of Hellen Hanks. In fact, the gossip had confused Keller's plight with the arrest of Bill Crook, a Valdosta insurance executive who had been taken into custody on June 24th on a charge of conspiracy to murder his wife.[b] Whatever the speculation, it had apparently remained confined to the local area. Only days before his arrest Keller had been reelected as secretary-treasurer of the Georgia Outdoor Advertising Association, a position he had held for several years.[55]

Keller Wilcox was not the only one arrested early on the morning of July 3rd. At an 8:00 A.M. news conference, Sheriff Carter, Chief Arnold, and District Attorney Lamar Cole announced the arrests of Foxy Wilcox, age seventy-three, and two black former employees of Wilcox Advertising, Ed Wrentz, age seventy-seven, and Lorenzo

---

[a] Wilby Coleman's wife was Hyta Mederer's step-daughter. Hyta Mederer was Keller Wilcox's maternal aunt.

[b] Willian E. Crook, aged fifty-two, and Vonda Kay Wisenbaker, his twenty-eight-year-old secretary, were arrested on murder conspiracy charges. Sheriff Robert Carter said the two were accused of attempting to hire someone to murder Crook's fifty-year-old wife, making it appear that she had been killed after surprising a burglar. On April 22, 1981, Mrs. Crook was shot and seriously wounded by an unknown assailant. She later appealed to a grand jury not to indict her husband. In an October 1981 trial Crook was found innocent, with his wife serving as the main witness for the defense (*Columbus* (GA) *Daily Enquirer*, June 26, 1981; *Augusta Chronicle*, August 2, 1981; *Brunswick* (GA) *News*, September 5, 1981).

Marshall, age sixty-nine. The three had been picked up on the charge of "hindering the apprehension of a criminal," specifically, "helping to remove and bury the victim."[56] The authorities revealed little more than the arrests, preferring instead to present their evidence at a committal hearing to be scheduled in the near future. They did admit they had "been zeroing in on the four men for weeks as prime suspects."[57] The hearing, to be held before a magistrate judge, would determine if the state's evidence was sufficient to warrant the presentation of the charges to a grand jury. Cole refused to say whether or not he would consider seeking the death penalty against Keller Wilcox.

Foxy Wilcox, Wrentz, and Marshall, charged with lesser offenses, were arraigned at the city jail before Justice of the Peace George Hart. The bail for each man was set at $25,000. Keller Wilcox, facing the more serious charge, was arraigned later in the morning before Superior Court Judge W. G. Elliot, who heard arguments from both the state and defense attorney Coleman. The judge set Keller's bail at $100,000. By midday, both of the Wilcoxes were free. Hyta Mederer, Foxy's sister-in-law and Keller's aunt, posted bond for both. The two black former employees remained behind bars.

The long investigation was over, and now the state faced the prospect of convincing a jury that those arrested were guilty of the crimes with which they were charged. The bizarre and sensational nature of the case quickly propelled it to the top of the news, both locally and regionally. On July 13th, ten days after the arrests of the suspects, the *Atlanta Constitution* featured a long front-page article covering the details of the alleged crimes, the backgrounds of those charged, and the local reaction to the shocking news. Dispatched to Valdosta to cover the case, the *Constitution*'s reporter interviewed John B. Lastinger, executive director of the Valdosta Chamber of Commerce and "a lifelong friend of the Wilcox family." Lastinger stated that he doubted the Wilcoxes' guilt. "Until they look me in the eye and tell me that he killed her and they buried her, I just won't believe they did it.... I've known Keller all his life," Lastinger continued. "I coached him in Little

League.... I can see where a father might do that to help his boy (out of trouble) but I just don't think Keller Wilcox has it in him to kill someone." On the other hand, Lastinger said, he'd known both the sheriff and the police chief for years as well. "Both lawmen know it would be political suicide to accuse members of the Wilcox family in these parts."

Lastinger, along with "about forty other Valdosta families," was at Fernandina Beach when word arrived of the Wilcoxes' arrests. "The news spread like wildfire among people on the beach," he recalled. "Speculation about the case had been circulating for months." Back in Valdosta, Wilby Coleman admitted, "For weeks rumors had been flying around town," opining that "the police got stampeded into making an arrest.... I think they went out and made themselves a case to take the heat off." Out on bail and back in his office, Foxy Wilcox told a reporter, "It's a harrowing experience having your only son arrested for murder. I hope you never have to go through it." Looking the visitor squarely in the eye, Foxy declared, "We are not guilty." Keller Wilcox refused to comment on the situation.

A committal hearing for the four men accused in Hellen Hanks's death was scheduled for July 24th, three weeks after their arrests. Three days prior to its start, a front-page headline on the afternoon edition of the *Valdosta Daily Times* announced that famed Georgia trial attorney Bobby Lee Cook had been retained to assist in the defense of Keller and Foxy. For the Wilcoxes, failure was not an option.

Chapter 8

The Man from Summerville

The December 13, 1981, issue of *Atlanta Weekly* magazine featured an article titled "The Jazz Justice of Bobby Lee Cook." Claiming that "he may be the most famous lawyer in Georgia," the writer noted, "He lives in a small town, but he's strictly big time. He's Shakespeare in legal clothing and a master of improvisation in the courtroom." It was a fawning piece, one of many such written about Cook over the years. This simple man from Summerville, Georgia, was seemingly capable of courtroom magic. As the author described him,

> *There is a perfect portrait yet to be painted of Bobby Lee Cook. His blue eyes would be focused at a point six inches past the back of your head, and he would be holding a pipe filled with Sir Walter Raleigh tobacco to his mouth. Smoke would billow and plume around his face, obscuring the rest of his features. The effect would be that of seeing a man without seeing him at all. That is how it is with great actors and great lawyers, you know they are capable of manipulating reality and of creating a world that could, but does not, exist. They know the plot and you don't; they parcel out a version of reality and ask you to believe it.*[58]

At age fifty-six and near the peak of his career, Cook had earned a formidable reputation as a defense attorney, an image carefully burnished by well-placed publicity, confirmed by a willingness to take on high-profile civil and criminal cases, and verified by a track record of often winning against heavy odds.

Bobby Lee Cook was born in 1925 near Lyerly, Georgia, a small town in the extreme northwestern part of the state a few miles from the Alabama border. A young man with ambition but not a lot of money, he briefly attended the Vanderbilt University Law School and later took classes at the University of Georgia School of Law, graduating from neither. He "read the law" and was able to pass the bar examination in 1949, as was possible in the day. After a brief stint in politics and a decade or more of small-town law practice characterized by an aggressive defense of those accused of serious crime, Cook's fame spread, as did his client base. Though still based in tiny Summerville, Georgia, by 1981 he was both wealthy and in demand, often arriving in his trademark chauffeured Rolls Royce, dressed in his seersucker suit and looking very much like the television character of Ben Matlock, for whom Cook was said to be the role model.[a] Over the coming years he would defend such high-profile individuals as Wayne Williams, the prime suspect in the Atlanta Child Murders of 1979 to 1981, and Jim Williams, whose murder trials formed the basis of John Berendt's *Midnight in the Garden of Good and Evil.* Cook was good at what he did, very good. A 1986 article in the *Los Angeles Times* boasted of his winning "90%" of some 300 murder cases he'd defended.[59] A 1989 feature in an American Bar Association journal referred to his preventing conviction for "more than 90 percent of the defendants in more than 350 cases Cook has tried."[60] If anyone could win acquittal of the charges against Keller and Foxy Wilcox, it would be Bobby Lee Cook.

The arrest of two members of one of Valdosta's more prominent families on murder-related charges had become prime fodder for gossip and casual conversation over barbecue and beer during the hot midsummer of 1981. The hiring of one of the state's most well-known—

---

[a] *Matlock* was a television series that aired on NBC and subsequently on ABC between 1986 and 1995. Andy Griffith played the lead character, Ben Matlock, a folksy defense attorney based in Atlanta, known for his prowess in the courtroom as well as his exorbitant up-front legal fees. Cook was known to coyly half deny this, for example, replying to an interviewer when asked, "That's what they say. I can neither confirm or deny. But I can tell you this—they used a lot of my cases." (https://www.superlawyers.com/georgia/article/the-bobby-lee-cook-show/9bf73fef-d07e-4ea7-8a8f-2e79e625c5ef.html. Accessed June 14, 2018.)

and sometimes feared—defense attorneys circulated on the rumor mills with a mixture of both admiration and disbelief. It was all speculation, of course. No one really knew what cards the prosecutors held; that would have to wait for the first hearing. Some said, "They must be guilty, or Converse Bright would have gotten them off." Converse Bright was a local defense attorney with a positive reputation for winning acquittal or negotiating a lighter sentence in criminal cases. Others likened the indictments to being newly diagnosed with a serious medical illness: "If you are sick, you want to go to a specialist."

Throughout the myriad conversations on the subject, there was the mostly unspoken issue of social and economic standing, a "them-versus-us" mentality. Keller Wilcox, the accused murderer, was said to be a member of the "class that can get away with it." Hellen Hanks, his alleged victim, was one of the "everyday people." One keen observer of Valdosta's social scene in the summer of 1981 recalled, "The well-to-do either thought he was innocent or wanted him to get away with it, and then there were those who wanted him prosecuted."

Lamar Cole, the district attorney and the man who would face the vaunted Bobby Lee Cook in the courtroom, was in many ways Cook's opposite. They both had roots in northwest Georgia; Cole was born in Dalton, about thirty-five miles from Cook's birthplace. While Cook set out to study the law, Cole at first worked as a draftsman before becoming bored and deciding to attend the University of Georgia as an English major at age twenty-seven. With the encouragement of his wife, he changed directions, graduating from Georgia's School of Law in 1967. For the first few years, he worked as an in-house attorney for the Langdale Company, where he met Hellen Hanks, who was also employed there at the time. After a brief stint in private practice, he ran for and won the position of district attorney of the Southern Judicial Circuit, an office he assumed in 1973.

Cole was familiar with Bobby Lee Cook's reputation, of course. He recalled one case in which he was attempting to negotiate a plea with a defendant's attorney. The lawyer said, "You better seriously consider my offer of a plea bargain, 'cause if you don't, the family's gonna hire Bobby Lee Cook."[61] Unlike Cook, however, Cole was generally unwilling to boast about his biggest cases. "Most involve murders," he explained to an interviewer. "Digging up the details means opening old wounds."[62] However skilled the attorney for the defense might be, it would be the evidence and hard facts that would in the end decide the outcome of the case.

Thus, the stage was set for the coming struggle, the first act of which would be a committal hearing to determine if the state's evidence was sufficient to warrant its referral to a grand jury. The contest had the potential to be a battle royal, a confrontation pitting an expensive, experienced, nationally known trial lawyer defending wealthy and socially prominent clients against a rural south Georgia district attorney seeking justice for the family of the murdered victim, a woman of modest means who struggled to support her family on a $120 weekly salary.

Chapter 9

The State Reveals Its Evidence

The committal hearing for the defendants in the Hellen Hanks murder case began at 9:00 A.M. on Friday, July 24, 1981, in the courtroom of the Lowndes County Courthouse in Valdosta.[63] The purpose was to hear what evidence the state possessed that supported the charges against the accused and to give the defendants' attorneys a chance to present their response. If confirmed, the cases would be bound over for consideration by a grand jury with the power to issue formal indictments. Such proceedings were normally held in the smaller grand jury room, but the notoriety of the case and the expected crowd of spectators called for a larger venue. Small Claims Court Judge E. Hulyn Smith presided. All four defendants and their attorneys were present: Bobby Lee Cook and Wilby Coleman represented the two Wilcoxes. Lamar Cole, as district attorney, represented the state. The Hanks family had hired a private special prosecutor, Dwight May, to assist Cole with the case.[a] May had formerly worked with the district attorney's office but was now in private practice in Moultrie, Georgia. Both of the black workers had been assigned court-appointed attorneys, Michael Bennett for Ed Wrentz and E. Cam Hickman for Lorenzo Marshall.

The hearing began with an unexpected twist. The state had applied for and received a grant of immunity for Ed Wrentz, who had become a witness for the prosecution. In exchange for his testimony,

---

[a] While the State of Georgia was the party formally prosecuting the charges against the defendants, legal practice in 1981 allowed those representing the victim—most commonly family members—to hire, at their own cost, an assistant special prosecutor.

charges against him would be dropped. Wrentz's attorney had agreed to the bargain, thus freeing his client from the risk of incarceration. Wrentz would be the first to testify.

Ed Wrentz was now seventy-eight years old.[b] He had originally begun his working career with Lewis Outdoor Advertising in 1924, continuing to work with the company after Foxy Wilcox purchased it in 1948 and changed the name.[c] He was still employed there on a part-time basis in 1972 when Hellen Hanks disappeared. Wrentz had only a third-grade education, was functionally illiterate, and had difficulty hearing. He often became confused during his testimony, frequently not understanding the questions posed to him on the stand. As such, he was not the ideal witness. Despite these limitations, the state's case would rely heavily on his testimony.

Cole's initial questioning of Wrentz was punctuated by frequent and repetitive objections from Bobby Lee Cook, with these interruptions making the district attorney's interrogation all the more difficult.[d] Cole began by asking if Wrentz recalled digging a hole. He replied that he did, at the direction of Foxy and Keller Wilcox, with the assistance of Lorenzo Marshall. As his testimony unfolded, bit by bit, Wrentz related that one evening some years earlier, he and Marshall had been

---

[b] Edward J. Wrentz was born on July 21, 1903, hence he was seventy-seven years old at the time of his arrest and seventy-eight years old at the time of the committal hearing.

[c] Lewis Advertising was chartered in 1926, according to documents on file in Lowndes County records. Assuming that Wrentz was correct in the 1924 date, it is quite possible that he was working for the Lewis family two years earlier.

[d] As a general statement regarding the questioning of witnesses in a court of law, the side for which the witness is testifying is allowed to ask broad questions but not to suggest preferred answers; e.g., "What did you see when you walked into the room?" as opposed to, "Did you see the defendant with a gun in his hand standing over the dead body when you walked into the room?" The latter question is an example of "leading the witness." On the other hand, when the opposite side is cross-examining the same witness, "leading" questions are permitted to a degree. There are many exceptions to this principle.

carried a few miles outside of Valdosta and instructed to dig a hole in the earth. They rode in the back of a "yellow pickup," driven by "Mr. Keller and Mr. Wilcox." Wrentz didn't know the exact location of the digging site but described it as being just off a dirt road in an area of bushes and scrub underbrush. It was near sunset, but there was still adequate light to work.[e] After digging about forty minutes, their efforts were interrupted by a heavy rain shower, so they stopped and were carried back to town.

Wrentz couldn't remember the exact details, but stated that within "the next day or two," they went back and finished digging the hole, again accompanied by Keller and Foxy Wilcox. When asked how deep the hole was, he stated that when standing in it, the level of the earth was up to about his waistline, somewhat less than three feet deep. After finishing, they returned to Wilcox Advertising to "get the box." When asked what was in the box, Wrentz replied, "A body."

"And whose body was it?" Cole asked.

"It was Mrs. Hanks," Wrentz replied, going on to testify that "me and Lorenzo" had put her body in the box.

Cole then asked, "And do your remember anything about Mrs. Hanks's legs?"

"Her legs?" Wrentz replied.

"Yes, sir."

"Well, there was some packages there that I guess was her legs."

"I see," Cole stated. "Did you take hold of her legs?"

"Yes, sir. I taken hold of her legs."

"Were they connected to her body?"

"No, sir," Wrentz said. "The legs was separate—separate."

"Separate from her body. And who put them in the box?"

"Well, me,"

"You did?"

---

[e] The sun set in Valdosta, Georgia, at 7:57 P.M. on August 31, 1972.

"Yes, sir."

"I see." Cole said again, then asked, "Who told you and Lorenzo to put that body in that box?"

"Mr. Keller and Mr. Wilcox," Wrentz replied.

Wrentz's testimony continued, describing the box that held Hellen Hanks's body as being the type used at Wilcox Advertising, designed to be placed on the back of a truck to hold posting paper. He said the box was "kind of a slate color." The four men took the box back to where they had dug the hole. Wrentz and Marshall "slid" it into the grave. Cole asked if there was anything else put in the grave along with the box. Wrentz replied affirmatively, saying, "It was like some clothes or a package or something."

Continuing the line of questioning, Wrentz was asked, "Did [Mrs. Hanks] have her clothes on, or did she not have clothes on?"

"She did not have her clothes on," Wrentz replied. Further questioning by Cole produced the admission that Wrentz did not report this to the police because he was "scared."

With the main points of the state's evidence established, Bobby Lee Cook began his cross-examination of the witness, continuing for more than two hours. While Wrentz's testimony about the details of digging a hole and burying a box containing the body of Hellen Hanks seemed clear enough when questioned by the district attorney, under vigorous interrogation by the defense his credibility suffered. At times appearing confused, Wrentz seemed unable to understand many of the questions posed by Cook, often repeating them without a specific answer. When asked about the year and month, he claimed it was November 1978, rather than July 1981. He mistakenly identified the prosecutor, Lamar Cole, as his lawyer, but a careful reading of the transcript seems to indicate that he did not understand the question. Having obtained this statement, Cook tried to get Wrentz to say that the prosecutor had instructed him as to what to say, implying that his account of Hellen Hanks's burial was fabricated. However, despite the distraction and confusion of the cross-examination, Wrentz's story remained basically the same: he and Lorenzo Marshall dug a hole and buried in it a box containing the body of Hellen Hanks, all this being done at the direction of, and with assistance from, Foxy and Keller Wilcox.

The other point of Cook's cross-examination was the manner in which the witness was questioned prior to his arrest. Apparently Wrentz was interviewed at police headquarters not long after the body was discovered, then a second and third time, the latter being on April 10, 1981. At first he admitted nothing to his interrogators despite being questioned for hours without the presence of an attorney or family members. As would be established in testimony later in the hearing, Wrentz recalled (or admitted) on April 10th that he had something to do with burying the box. He told investigators of the role of the Wilcoxes and that "another black man" whose name he could not remember assisted him.[64] The break in the case came with Wrentz's fourth and final meeting with the police on July 2nd. It was then that he named Lorenzo Marshall as the other person who helped dig the makeshift grave. The four defendants were taken into custody shortly thereafter.

With the attorneys for both the prosecution and the defense having completed their examination of Ed Wrentz, Judge Smith announced that he wanted to question the witness himself. Turning to Wrentz he explained, "From the testimony and the questions you have been asked this morning, the answers are not completely clear in my mind." In response to the judge's questions, Wrentz admitted that he and Lorenzo Marshall dug a hole that would be used as a grave. They put a body that he recognized as being that of Mrs. Hanks in a box. He said that the legs had been severed from the body at the knees and that Foxy and Keller Wilcox were present and drove the truck that took the two men to dig the hole and subsequently bury the box.

Following Ed Wrentz's testimony, James Hanks was questioned briefly regarding the events of the evening his wife disappeared. His testimony was followed by that of Dr. Robert Jackson, a local dentist who had done Hellen Hanks's dental restoration work between 1970 and 1972. It was Dr. Jackson who identified the body based on a comparison of his dental records and the deceased woman's upper jaw. Cook, in cross-examination, questioned him harshly, with criticism for such things as failing to "make any scientific analyses or attempt to make any scientific analyses of any metallographic findings of the dental alloy." Dr. Jackson stood by his identification stating, in essence, that such was not necessary in this case.

The final testimony was given by Lieutenant Billy Selph of the Lowndes County Sheriff's Department (LCSD) regarding the evidence recovered from the burial site. Selph was present at the investigation of the scene by local authorities, with the assistance of the state crime laboratory team from Moultrie. He also participated in the questioning of both Ed Wrentz and Lorenzo Marshall. In this regard, Lamar Cole moved to introduce a copy of Lorenzo Marshall's statement given on the evening of July 2nd. Following Ed Wrentz's identification of Marshall as the other man who helped dig the hole and bury the body, Marshall, with encouragement by the police, agreed to give a voluntary written statement of his involvement. Over the objections of the defense attorneys, and after discussion as to the evidentiary value of Marshall's statement, Selph was allowed to read it into the record:

> *On the day that Mrs. Hanks went missing, Keller and Mr. Wilcox both told me about Mrs. Hanks going missing. I don't remember exactly when, but Ed Wrentz came to me and asked me to help him dig a hole and I went along. Me and Ed went back to the Wilcox Company and met up with Keller Wilcox and we got into his truck and Keller carried us out to where we was to dig a hole. Keller showed us where to dig and we dug. We carried a shovel and something else; I don't remember what it was. We had to clear away some bushes before we started digging. Me and Ed dug the hole about the same amount. I got down in the hole and it was about waist deep. When we started to digging the hole it started raining and we loaded up and left. I don't remember if it was the next day or not but we went back and finished the hole. We went back to the business and Keller and Mr. Wilcox was*

> *there. Keller backed up the truck into the warehouse and told us to load the box up and we did. The box was in the warehouse. All four of us went back to the same place where we had dug the hole, me and Ed put the box in the hole and covered it up. The reason I helped Ed was because I knew him good. When the hole was dug and the box was put in it Keller was there and I knew that what we was doing was for the Wilcoxes. I seen Ed throw something in the hole before the box was put in the hole, it looked like a dress. I did not know what was in the box.*

Between Marshall's statement and Wrentz's testimony, the state had strong evidence that both Keller and Foxy Wilcox were responsible for placing Hellen Hanks's body in a box and subsequently burying the box in a remote location, assuming that it never would be found. However, there were clearly disparities in the testimony, notably Lorenzo Marshall's allegation that he did not know the contents of the box he and Ed Wrentz were burying. On the other hand, that could easily be explained as a self-serving statement on Marshall's part, hoping to avoid a charge of being complicit in her murder.

Lamar Cole made a brief closing argument for the state. He pointed out, based on testimony given at the hearing, that there was reasonable evidence to charge Keller Wilcox with Hellen Hanks's murder, and Foxy Wilcox, Ed Wrentz, and Lorenzo Marshall with hiding her body and failing to report the crime. Specifically, Keller was the first and only person seen at Wilcox Advertising when James Hanks arrived on the scene. Second, the body was positively identified as that of Hellen Hanks. Third, the box in which she was buried was consistent with that type used at Wilcox Advertising. Finally, Wrentz's testimony and Marshall's sworn statement implicated both Keller and Foxy Wilcox in the attempt to hide the body.

Cole acknowledged that the actual cause of death could not be determined, and without this knowledge a charge of murder might be questioned. Admitting the state's charges were based on circumstantial evidence, he explained, "It might be said that it hasn't been shown here today that [Keller Wilcox] struck the fatal blow, but, Your Honor, she was dead, and if she wasn't when she was buried, she got that way after she was buried, and that could be murder. And why else would he have his old, trusted employee bury a dismembered body if he hadn't done the crime?"

Bobby Lee Cook, in his closing argument, seemed to express disbelief that the case was even presented for a determination of probable cause. "Frankly..., in thirty-two years of law practice throughout this state and throughout this country, I say this to the court with the utmost candor and honesty, that I have never seen a homicide case presented...in this manner in which any request was made to bind anyone over to the Grand Jury for probable cause."

Describing Lamar Cole as "a bright, articulate young man," before criticizing the state's case, Cook went on to say, "There is no evidence—there is not a scintilla or scratch of evidence before this Court that Keller Wilcox or any individual here has caused the death of Mrs. Hanks. There is not a shred of evidence to that effect. There is no evidence before this Court, and had there been evidence in existence, it was the duty and the responsibility of the District Attorney of this circuit to produce it." Citing the sometimes contradictory testimony of Ed Wrentz and the absence of actual knowledge of the way in which Hellen Hanks died, Cook suggested that the Court dismiss the charges for lack of evidence directly tying his clients to her death.

After a brief statement by Cam Hickman, Lorenzo Marshall's attorney, also requesting that the charges against his client be dismissed, Judge Smith ruled without further comment: "The defendants, Keller Wilcox, E. K. Wilcox, Senior, and Lorenzo Marshall are hereby bound over to the Lowndes County Grand Jury."

Chapter 10

Waiting for the Other Shoe to Drop

With the case referred to a grand jury, the prospect of the defendants facing trial seemed inevitable. The local paper reported that between thirty-five and fifty onlookers had attended the eight-hour committal hearing on Friday, July 24th. Among them were two of Hellen Hanks's brothers, Herman and "Doc" Griffin of Jesup and Nashville, Georgia, respectively. Both expressed their dissatisfaction with the missing person inquiry in 1972 but said they were "well pleased" with the current investigation after the discovery of their sister's remains.[65]

On Sunday, July 26th, the *Valdosta Daily Times* ran a four-column, front-page article on "The Hanks Case," with the subtitle, "A Look at the Families Involved in Sensational Murder Case." Under photos of Ed Wrentz, the Wilcoxes, and Hellen Hanks, the paper's city editor reviewed the basic facts of the story thus far in a chatty piece, describing the background of the "principal characters," to use his term. The Hanks family was described as hard-working, church-going, salt-of-the-earth folk. The Wilcoxes, on the other hand, were said to be "members of an old-line Valdosta family which moves easily in top social circles." Describing them as being financially "comfortable," the editor averred that, "The Wilcox standing in the community's social structure doesn't depend on money. 'Membership,' as one member of the invisible but fairly clearly defined class said, is based on 'family background, grace and such things, but not money.'" "Fact and fiction," the article continued, "are hard to separate in the case. Small talk from the coffee shops to the country club to the beer joints eventually settles on the Hanks case these days around Valdosta. The case has pretty much polarized opinion here into two groups. A jury of twelve men and women who have not formed some opinion on the case would be hard to find, if not impossible, in Lowndes County. It would be hard to find such an insulated jury panel in Georgia since the case has drawn statewide press coverage."[66]

Public interest aside, both the prosecution and defense teams faced an uncertain future. An indictment by the September grand jury seemed a certainty, barring the discovery of new and unexpected exculpatory evidence. If Wrentz and Marshall were to be believed, the state had excellent testimony to support the defendants' charge of improperly disposing of a body. But the murder charge against Keller Wilcox was based primarily on circumstantial evidence since the precise cause and manner of Hellen Hanks's death were unknown. Assuming the case would make it to trial, a clean jury verdict of guilty or not guilty on the question of murder would necessarily require a leap of faith on the part of the panel. The state's major goal would be presenting evidence and testimony that would help the jury bridge the gaps in the narrative. On the opposite side, the defendants' attorneys would need to focus on these same unknowns, in the process convincing jurors that there were other, perhaps equally plausible, scenarios that could account for the known facts and evidence.

Meanwhile, both the state and the defense attorneys were preparing their cases. For the prosecution, the thorniest issue was the exact cause of Hellen Hanks's death. The State Crime Laboratory in Atlanta had received her skeletal remains on December 5, 1980, but the final report on the lab's findings was not released until June 18, 1981, some six and a half months later. The lab director's secretary had temporarily misplaced the initial draft, causing the delay. Based on the skeletal remains sent to the lab, it was impossible to determine how she died.

The other uncertain issue was Ed Wrentz's testimony that Hellen Hanks's body had been dismembered. This was in some respects a surprise to investigators, as neither the local investigators nor the state crime lab had initially found evidence of this. Part of the problem may well have been the disturbance of the initial position of the bones within the box caused by the root rake and the Blantons' attempt to jerk the box out of the ground. Only those who directly participated in disposing of the body would know that the legs had been severed, and at trial this would have important bearing on the state's case. If that part of Ed Wrentz's testimony could not be proven, then the rest of his account of Hellen Hanks's burial could be cast in doubt.

After discussing the options with Dr. Larry B. Howard, director of the crime lab, the decision was made to exhume Hellen Hanks's remains from the Morven cemetery for a careful reexamination of her leg bones in an effort to objectively verify Wrentz's testimony. This was done quietly on August 17th on orders from Lowndes County Coroner Harold Moore and Brooks County Coroner Hugh Bassham, responding to a formal request from Dr. Howard. The bones of the legs and a bone from one of the victim's arms were taken for examination, while the rest of the skeletal remains were reburied two days later. Defense attorneys were not formally notified of the disinterment; Bobby Lee Cook would later state that he had learned of it "through the grapevine."[67]

After examining the bones of both knee joints, Dr. Howard took them to Maryland to consult with Dr. Ellis R. Kerley, a professor at the University of Maryland and a nationally known specialist in forensic anthropology. Both agreed there were findings consistent with the lower legs having been cut from the body at or near the time of death. This time Dr. Howard's report was delivered to the investigators eight days after receiving the remains.

On September 4th, a Lowndes County Grand Jury composed of six men and fourteen women indicted Keller Wilcox on charges of murder and of concealing a death.[a] Foxy Wilcox and Lorenzo Marshall

---

[a] The same grand jury indicted William Crook, the insurance executive, on charges of "criminal solicitation," more specifically, attempting to hire a hit man to kill his wife. The wife, Anita Crook, had been shot by an unknown assailant in April 1981 but survived. She testified before the grand jury, asking them not to indict her husband. Her husband's attorneys stated that she was expected to testify on his behalf at his trial. Charges against William Crook's twenty-eight-

were each indicted on charges of concealing a death and hindering apprehension and punishment of a criminal. Formal arraignment was scheduled for September 18th, two weeks later.[b]

The arraignment hearings for the Wilcoxes and Lorenzo Marshall were held at the Lowndes County jail before Superior Court Judge George A. Horkan. Foxy and Keller were represented by Wilby Coleman, and in a separate hearing Marshall was represented by Cam Hickman. The proceedings were brief and to the point. All the defendants pled not guilty. Dates for hearing pretrial motions were set. Marshall's trial was scheduled for October 5th. In view of what the court expected to be a large number of pretrial motions for the Wilcox cases, the trial date was tentatively set for November 2nd. Superior Court Judge Roy M. Lilly of Thomasville, Georgia, would be presiding. Lamar Cole had still not announced if he would be seeking the death penalty for Keller.

Little had been heard publicly from Foxy and Keller Wilcox since their arrests and indictments. In mid-September, a reporter for the *Tampa Bay Times* paid a visit to Valdosta for the purpose of writing a feature article on the murder.[68] The paper's interest sprang from the fact that Keller was a graduate of Admiral Farragut Academy, located in the St. Petersburg, Florida, home of the *Times*. He met with the Wilcoxes, interviewed Wilby Coleman and others around town, and in the process painted a somewhat upbeat portrait of two men facing what could only be described as devastating criminal charges.

The *Times*'s reporter, Bill Cornwall, described Foxy as "a large, pear-shaped man, with hair as bristly as a wet squirrel's fur. His face is long and accentuated by Lyndon Johnson-like ears, and while he walks with a shuffle that is not uncommon for men of his years, his mind

---

year-old secretary had been dropped at a preliminary hearing (*Atlanta Constitution*, September 5, 1981).

[b] In 1981, the crime of concealing a death was classed as a misdemeanor. Georgia law has subsequently been changed to upgrade this offense to a felony. Perhaps needless to say, the crime of murder is considered a felony.

seems sharp and clear." As for Keller, Cornwall reported that, "At 30, he retains the clean-cut good looks that those who knew him at Admiral Farragut recall. Dressed in a blue blazer with gold buttons, striped shirt and tie, tan slacks and highly polished loafers, he looks like any number of young men from well-to-do families who return to small towns to help run their daddies' businesses."

As for their day-to-day activities, Cornwall wrote,

> *Foxy and his son Keller are two of the most prominent residents of this city of about 40,000 people, and they aren't about to let something like the most sensational murder case in south Georgia's recent history keep them down. So they continue to go to their Rotary Clubs, continue to remain involved in the Boys Club, continue to operate their successful outdoor advertising business and continue to indulge their shared passions for football and fishing.*
>
> *"I don't have anything to be ashamed of," explains Keller.... "After the first day or two (following his arrest for murder on July 3), life has been normal."*
>
> *"I have continued my daily activities," chimes in 73-year-old Foxy from behind a cloud of pipe tobacco smoke.*
>
> *While Foxy and Keller go about their business, just about everybody else in Valdosta talks about how horrible it is for a fine family to be involved in such a mess, reads every newspaper article that is printed on the subject, and wonders, "Are the Wilcoxes guilty?"*

Asked for his thoughts, Wilby Coleman insisted his clients "are just as damn innocent as the driven snow. The state had no evidence." Captain Billy Selph of the Lowndes County Sheriff's Department countered with, "We've got a very good case, and that's all I'm going to say."

In what would be a telling statement, Foxy Wilcox was quoted as saying, "The possibility (of conviction) is there, but in all probability, the jury is going to look at the evidence, and, in my opinion, we have evidence that will vouch for our whereabouts and actions that day." He also admitted that "when he was arrested, he had two airline tickets, one for Keller, one for himself, in his pocket—a circumstance that he did not publicize. 'What if the newspapers had known that I had two tickets to Canada in my pocket, wouldn't that have made a good story?'" Ostensibly, the tickets were for a fishing trip.

Chapter 11

A Sex Crime

If the state couldn't prove *how* Hellen Hanks was killed, then it had to explain *why*, and in some way connect that reason to Keller Wilcox, the accused. From the outset, members of law enforcement described her death as "a sex crime," but released little specific information to support this contention. Based on the findings when her body was discovered, she was nude at the time of her burial, and "her clothes had been torn and ripped from her body."[69] Seeking an expert opinion, investigators contacted Dr. Park Elliott Dietz, a practicing psychiatrist and at the time a faculty member at Harvard Medical School.

In 1981, at just thirty-three years of age, Dr. Dietz was relatively unknown, though highly qualified. A Phi Beta Kappa graduate of Cornell University, he earned his MD and master's degrees from Johns Hopkins University. He would later go on to become one of America's most prominent forensic psychiatrists. Over the coming years, Dietz would consult or testify in many of the nation's high-profile criminal cases, including those of John W. Hinckley Jr., Jeffery Dahmer, the "Unabomber" terrorist Ted Kaczynski, and Andrea Yates, to name a few.

On September 26th, Dietz met for four and a half hours with Sergeant Charlie Spray and Detective Lieutenant Billy Selph at the Embassy Row Hotel in Washington, DC. The officers briefed him on the case and brought with them physical evidence found with the victim's remains, including "a piece of rope and the remains of a woman's dress, half-slip, brassiere, panties, girdle and pantyhose."[70] He also viewed photographs of the gravesite, the Wilcox Advertising premises, and the skull identified as belonging to Hellen Hanks. In a damning letter to Lamar Cole, Dietz wrote,

In my opinion, the physical evidence recovered from the gravesite is strongly indicative of a sexually motivated homicide or of a death disguised to appear like a sexually motivated homicide. I use the term sexually motivated homicide to include murders committed for the purpose of deriving sexual satisfaction from (1) the victim's pain and suffering (sexual sadism), (2) the act of killing per se and/or acts of violence, domination or exploration committed upon the corpse (lust murder), (3) explicitly sexual activity with the corpse (necrophilia), or (4) any combination of these. A sexually motivated homicide does not necessarily include penetration, though this may occur before and/or after death.

It is the fact that the piece of rope I examined appears to have been the murder weapon that leads me to doubt that this was a murder committed to escape detection for rape. A rapist seeking to quiet his victim is unlikely to kill her with a rope and more likely to employ manual throttling or whatever other weapon he had used to intimidate his victim (e.g., a knife, blunt instrument, or gun).

It is possible but highly improbable that the victim died in a manner other than homicide and was sexually abused after death.

Another possible but highly improbable set of events is that the victim engaged in consensual sadomasochistic sexual activities which included the cutting of her dress and brassiere, that the manner of her death was accident, suicide or natural, and that an attempt was made to conceal her death. The possibility would only be plausible if evidence existed that the victim had previously engaged voluntarily in sadomasochistic sexual activity.

If you were to reenact a series of events which might result in a dead woman, a kinked piece of rope, and a dress and brassiere cut in the manner observed, I believe you would find the most straightforward solution to the "riddle" is that she was strangled from behind, using the rope as a ligature, and that her clothing was removed when she was dead or unconscious. The cutting of the dress and the brassiere indicates that the victim's upper extremities were tied (behind her, at the sides, or in front of her) or that he assailant expected to derive pleasure from the cutting of her clothing, or both. Tying up and the tearing or cutting of clothing are common in the fantasies and behavior of sexual sadists.[71]

If asked to serve as an expert witness, Dr. Dietz agreed to testify at Keller Wilcox's trial.

In preparation for the hearings scheduled in early October, both the defense and prosecution filed a number of motions. Among the more than a dozen filed by the defense were requests for a change of venue, citing the extensive reporting on the Hanks case, a motion for separate trials for the accused, a motion to suppress Lorenzo Marshall's statement, and a request for a competency hearing for Ed Wrentz based on his erratic testimony at the committal hearing. There were motions to bar testimony from Keller Wilcox's ex-wife, Jean, as well as testimony that he sexually harassed Hellen Hanks prior to her disappearance. The defense moved to exhume the victim's remains for a third time so that their expert could examine them for findings that the state crime laboratory and/or the prosecution's expert might have missed. There was a motion—considered standard—to bar the state from seeking the death penalty. As expected, the defense filed a Brady motion, demanding that the prosecution turn over to the defense all evidence in its possession, including witness testimony, which might be favorable or exculpatory for the accused.[a]

Lamar Cole, representing the state, made the decision not to pursue the death penalty for Keller Wilcox, a relief to the defense. He did, however, file a motion seeking a psychiatric examination for Wilcox, noting, "The state anticipates that the defendant may utilize at trial the defense of insanity." As support for the motion he cited "the condition of the body and other evidence in the case 'suggests that Mrs. Hanks was the victim of a sexually related or deviantly motivated scheme of mind.'"[72]

---

[a] A so-called "Brady motion," based on the United States Supreme Court case of *Brady v. Maryland* (1963), is filed prior to a trial and designed to force prosecutors to reveal all witnesses and evidence they hold in pursuing a criminal conviction, especially when that witness or evidence may favor the defendant or weaken the prosecution's case.

Wilby Coleman responded,

> *"I am just totally stunned at Lamar's gall, filing a motion such as this." He accused the district attorney of filing the motion as "a ploy to the public, through the media," to plant the idea in the public mind that his client is capable of killing. "The defense is that he (Wilcox) simply didn't do it," Coleman said. "There will be no defense of insanity whatsoever." He said his client "is a walking-around, certified normal human being who is on the board of directors of the Boys Club and the Chamber of Commerce." Coleman said Wilcox had never seen a psychiatrist for any reason, and the defense would vigorously fight the motion for a psychiatric examination.*[73]

To a reporter for a Jacksonville, Florida, newspaper, "Coleman said Cole's recent loss of another case in which a Valdosta insurance man was found innocent of trying to hire someone to kill his wife might have played a role in the motion for a psychiatric examination.[b] 'He lost that one and he wants to win this one.'"[74]

The hearings on the pretrial motions began as scheduled on Monday, October 12, 1981, lasting well into the next day. Judge Roy M. Lilly presided in the courtroom of the Lowndes County jail. The prosecution and defense each presented their various motions; some were granted, others rejected, and others deferred for further consideration or to be decided at the time of trial. Action on the motion for a change of venue was deferred until the time of jury selection after the defense attorneys had an opportunity to assess possible preexisting bias in the jury pool. The motion for separate trials for the defendants was granted, but the motion for a psychiatric examination of Keller Wilcox was rejected, apparently on the basis of the failure to file it in a timely manner.

With regret, Judge Lilly granted the defense's request to exhume Hellen Hanks's remains for a third time. "I am most reluctant to

---

[b] Coleman is referring to the case of William E. Crook, who had been acquitted a few days prior to the Wilcox hearing. (See footnote page 56.)

disturb these remains again out of respect to the family and out of respect to the deceased herself," Lilly said. "I abhor it. But I am required, it seems to me, by the law...to permit the examination of the entire skeletal remains of the deceased in this case."[75] The defense planned to have its own expert, Dr. Joseph Burton, chief medical examiner for DeKalb and Cobb counties, examine the remains for identity, cause of death, and his opinion on whether or not the body had been dismembered.

The trial, which had been scheduled to begin on November 2nd, was deferred by Judge Lilly to January 4, 1982. Foxy Wilcox, slated to be a key witness at Keller's trial, was suffering from phlebitis and under a doctor's care, according the Wilby Coleman. He would be unable to testify for six to eight weeks.

The trial delay was perhaps inevitable. And there would be, without doubt, further motions and hearings before the two sides presented their cases to the jury. The hearing on the pretrial motions thus far had provided hints about each side's strategy. For the prosecution, the testimony of both Ed Wrentz and Lorenzo Marshall would be crucial. There likely would be testimony that Keller Wilcox had sexually harassed Hellen Hanks before her disappearance and that her death was somehow related to this. The defense's case would hinge on casting doubt on the state's case by discrediting the prosecution's witnesses and providing an alibi for the Wilcoxes' whereabouts when the victim vanished. Both sides faced a difficult task ahead. Only one side could prevail.

Chapter 12

Last-Minute Things

On December 21st attorneys for the defense and prosecution assembled once again for a hearing before Judge Lilly in the courtroom of the Lowndes County Courthouse. The majority of the proceeding was devoted to a motion to suppress the testimony of Jean Johannessen, Keller Wilcox's ex-wife.[a] The defense concerns focused on the fact that during the investigation of the Hanks case, Johannessen had been hypnotized, a process that might have somehow altered her memories of the events of August 1972.

Over several hours of testimony, four police officers were questioned, two of whom had attempted to hypnotize Mrs. Johannessen. Detective Lieutenant Billy Selph of the Lowndes County Sheriff's Department was the first called to the stand, followed by Staff Sergeant Charlie Spray, Detective Captain Billy Register, and Patrolman Jim Lawson of the Valdosta Police Department. Between December 1980 and mid-summer of 1981, Johannessen had been interviewed at least three times by members of law enforcement. On two occasions, once in the mid-spring, and later around the first of July, attempts had been made to hypnotize her. The stated goal was to help her recall facts and events that otherwise might have been suppressed in her memory.

Both Spray and Register had received very limited formal training in hypnosis. On examination, Bobby Lee Cook attacked their qualifications. Both had attended a one-week course held at the American Hotel in Atlanta in the late summer or early fall of 1978. The course

---

[a] The formal term for such is a "motion in limine," asking the judge in advance to suppress certain information that might be brought up at trial. The phrase "*in limine*" is Latin for "at the threshold" or "at the start."

was given by the Law Enforcement Hypnosis Institute and supposedly qualified its graduates to place potential witnesses under hypnosis, most commonly for the purpose of revealing details of events that might have otherwise been forgotten.

Register had first tried to hypnotize Johannessen but was unsuccessful. Spray did succeed in placing her in a hypnotic trance for about an hour during the mid-summer interview session. She had been cooperative with the investigators and had already told them all that she remembered before undergoing hypnosis. When asked if any new information was revealed, those present for the session agreed that little more was learned, only "minute" details. Each of the officers questioned said definitively that no recordings or notes were made of any of the interview sessions, including both attempts at hypnosis.

In pursuing a motion to suppress any testimony from his client's ex-wife, Cook vigorously attacked the use of hypnosis in potential witnesses. Quoting a statement from a consultant in an Arizona legal case in which the process was in dispute, Cook read,

> *I believe that once a potential witness has been hypnotized for the purpose of enhancing memory, his recollections have been so contaminated that he is rendered effectively incompetent to testify. Hypnotized persons being extremely suggestive wrap into their memories fantasies or suggestions deliberately or unwillingly [sic] communicated by the hypnotist. After hypnosis the subject cannot differentiate between a true recollection and a fantasy or a suggestive detail. Neither can [an] expert nor the trier of fact. The risk is so great that the use of hypnosis by police on a potential witness is tantamount to the destruction or fabrication of evidence.*[76]

Speaking for the prosecution, Lamar Cole objected strenuously, but Judge Lilly basically agreed with the defense, stating, "It's the Court's feeling that it would be a dangerous practice to permit persons to be placed under hypnosis and suggestions be made as to the...prospective witness, then use evidence which was disclosed following hypnosis. I think it would be a dangerous practice, I think it would be dangerous to submit it—that sort of evidence—to the jury."[77] Despite his thoughts at the time, Lilly said that he would defer a final ruling on the matter until after he had reviewed further information to be submitted by each side.

The remainder of the hearing was devoted to discussions regarding the defense's requests for various records and other evidence and whether or not the prosecution had fulfilled these requests, as required by the court. Several issues remained undecided at the end of the hearing.

The attorneys assembled once again in the courthouse before Judge Lilly nine days later on December 30th. Both sides had remained busy over the Christmas holiday, devising strategy, refining previous motions, and crafting new ones. New Year's Day was two days away; trial proceedings were still scheduled to get underway on January 4th, five days hence. Both sides agreed that the Brady motion requests had been satisfied. All of the relevant material held by the prosecution had been turned over to the defense team. The greatest surprise was the revelation of the existence of tape recordings of the three interviews with Jean Johannessen, despite the denials of all four police officers at the December 21st hearing. Copies of the tapes had been turned over to the defense on Christmas Eve.

The tape recordings opened a new opportunity for the defense to attack the state's case and perhaps delay the trial. An expert, Dr. Harry Hollien, had been called in to examine the tapes. Dr. Hollien was a faculty member and professor at the University of Florida in Gainesville. In addition to having earned two master's degrees and his doctorate, he was an internationally recognized authority in the field of "phonetic sciences." Having done a preliminary examination on part of the tape-recorded material, Dr. Hollien expressed his opinion that the tapes themselves were presumably original, but "there are a number of...areas that are quite suggestive of some manipulation which may or may not prove to be areas of manipulation for which I obviously would have to investigate."[78] Assuming that he would need at least ten hours to assess each hour of recording, he estimated that it would take him two to three weeks to complete the task. Cook proposed a motion for a postponement of the trial for at least three weeks beyond the scheduled January 4th start date. And if this were not enough, Cook raised an additional request that their forensic expert, Dr. Joseph Burton, be allowed to examine the clothing found in the grave with Hellen Hanks's remains, describing this "of critical importance to the defense" and perhaps another reason to delay the trial.

In response, District Attorney Cole pointed out that the tapes had not been entered into evidence, calling them "just a method of making a memorandum for the officers." Cook in turn replied that if evidence were found that the tapes had been "tampered with, fabricated, altered or modified," it would negatively reflect on "the credibility" of Officers Selph and Register, both of whom were expected to be key witnesses for the prosecution.

Judge Lilly, taking the motions and arguments of both sides into consideration, pointed out that there had already been substantial delays in bringing the matter to trial. While there remained some issues yet to be resolved, these could be addressed during the formal trial proceedings. Jury selection was to start as scheduled on January 4, 1982.

Chapter 13

The Trial—Days 1 and 2: Voir Dire

The opportunity of a trial by a jury of one's peers is one of the most fundamental of American rights. The concept finds its roots in ancient times and is considered a basic tenant of all free societies. The Declaration of Independence listed King George III's depravation of this right as one of the justifications for rebellion. The right to a jury trial is enshrined in Article III, Section 2 of the United States Constitution of 1789 and further clarified and expanded in the Bill of Rights' Sixth Amendment. Numerous court opinions have further defined the details of when and how trials are to be conducted. These are to be public events; the accused has a right to counsel and the right to confront those who would be witnesses against him. Most fundamentally, the accused is considered innocent until proven guilty.

With that said, jury trials are imperfect events. A group of laymen (or more properly, laypersons) is asked to seek the truth among what are often disparate and incomplete sets of "facts," decide on the veracity of conflicting testimony given by sworn witnesses, and reconstruct as nearly as possible unseen events that constituted a crime. Based on these premises, the jury must make a decision, rendering a verdict chosen from the binary options of guilt or non-guilt.[a]

Jurors are human beings and, as such, suffer from the foibles of the human condition. They are instructed to be objective, but there is

---

[a] To be correct, a jury does not find an accused "innocent." The proper term is "not guilty." Verdicts are rendered based on evidence and witness testimony presented at trial. In jury deliberations, these must be sufficient to prove guilt beyond a reasonable doubt. Otherwise, the verdict would be one of non-guilt. In popular parlance, however, this latter verdict is often spoken of as confirming the accused's innocence.

little doubt that personality and emotions play a role in how they react and respond to the evidence and testimony presented at trial. The right to a jury of one's peers does not mean that the panel will be comprised of those exactly similar to the accused. For that reason, the act of choosing jurors from a group of candidates has become a fine art, with both the prosecution and defense given limited rights to interview and sometimes arbitrarily reject potential jurors whom they feel might be inclined to vote against their side of the case.

The trial of the State of Georgia vs. E. Keller Wilcox Jr. began on the morning of Monday, January 4, 1982, amidst widespread public interest. The *Valdosta Daily Times* ran a long article in the previous day's Sunday edition reviewing the basics of the case and the people involved. Court officials were said to be predicting a trial of two to three weeks. The state had submitted a list of seventy-five potential witnesses in addition to a "lengthy" list from the defense lawyers. A jury pool of 125 had been called up. "Authorities said they intend to try and prove it was a sexually motivated crime," the article said, while noting, "Wilcox and his father have denied knowledge of the crime and contend they were out of town the day Mrs. Hanks disappeared." The narratives to be offered the jury by the prosecution and the defense could not have been more different, it would seem.

At 9:30 A.M., Judge Roy Lilly called the court to order to begin voir dire, the screening of the potential jurors.[b] Given the controversial nature of the case, he estimated that jury selection would occupy two days. Testimony was scheduled to begin on Wednesday, the 6th. Both the prosecution and defense were required to submit, in advance,

---

[b] Voir dire (from French, "to see to speak" in literal translation, but with more complicated etymological roots) is the term used to describe the screening of jurors by a judge and/or attorneys to determine potential bias prior to a court proceeding. The term is also used to refer to the questioning of alleged expert witnesses outside of the presence of a jury in order to assess qualifications and competency, and in similar situations.

questions that could potentially be posed to jurors. Many of these were simple (address, employment, relationship to the defendant, etc.), but others more probing. Lilly approved ten of the eleven questions submitted by the state, but rejected fifty of the seventy-three proposed by the defense. It was clear that Keller Wilcox's lawyers wanted to know as much as possible about the thought processes of the would-be jury panel.

Judge Lilly began by swearing in the entire group of those called for jury duty then explained the process in detail. The jury would be sequestered in a local hotel, he announced. In reviewing the jury's obligations, he emphasized,

> *Every person is presumed innocent until proven guilty. No person shall be convicted of a crime unless each element of the crime is proved beyond a reasonable doubt. The burden of proof rests upon the State to prove each essential element of the offense charged beyond a reasonable doubt. The State, however, is not required to prove the guilt of the defendant beyond all doubt. Moral and reasonable certainty is all that can be expected in a legal investigation.*

The proceedings, followed closely by the press, went smoothly. Lamar Cole first questioned each potential juror, followed by Bobby Lee Cook, occasionally punctuated by "minor clashes between Cook and Cole."[79] A reporter described the famous defense attorney as

> *a tall, thin, almost gaunt figure with a white beard wearing wire-rimmed glasses pushed down low on his nose. It's hard to look at him without thinking of Abraham Lincoln as a blond, but his name isn't Lincoln. It's Cook—Bobby Lee Cook. His name is well-known in criminal law circles. He's polite as he questions the jurors and tries to work in a folksy touch within the boundaries of courtroom decorum. Something in his manner, however, or maybe in his gaze, lets you know he's no bumpkin.*[80]

Cole, a local and by no means a celebrity, was not described.

The process moved slowly; by the end of the day on Monday, only thirty-five potential jurors had been screened. On Tuesday morning, the courtroom was filled once again as the questioning continued. Keller Wilcox was in attendance, quietly watching "without expression as a jury was chosen to decide if he did, indeed, kill Hellen Hanks and bury her dismembered body in that box."[81] A correspondent for the *Atlanta Constitution* observed,

> *Keller Wilcox has chamber-of-commerce good looks. His sandy hair is carefully cut. His fawn-colored suede blazer hangs well. His pin-striped shirt is starched; his tie is crisp; his Weejun loafers are shined. At 30, he's still boyishly handsome, if slightly pudgy from prosperity. He has an engaging grin, but never flashes it in the courtroom.*[82]

A number of jurors were released based on firm opinions about the guilt or innocence of the accused or other potential conflicts. At least three who admitted that they believed they had formed an opinion as to innocence or guilt based on what they had heard or read of the case were added to the jury panel over Bobby Lee Cook's objections. Judge Lilly pointed out that their opinions were based on hearsay evidence, and all stated they were willing to approach the final question of guilt or innocence based on what was presented at trial.

By early Tuesday afternoon, a panel of twelve jurors and two alternates had been chosen. Among the twelve—four men and eight women—were a retired farmer, a high school math teacher, a chemical company worker, a telephone operator, and the wife of a professor at Valdosta State College. Ten were white; two—both women—were black. In choosing the twelve, the state used eight of its ten strikes, while the defense used nineteen of its twenty.[c]

---

[c] During voir dire, attorneys for both the prosecution and defense are allowed to arbitrarily "strike" or dismiss potential jurors who might otherwise qualify. The reasoning here is based on the theory that some members of a jury pool may be more or less likely to act on hidden biases against one side or another in rendering a verdict. Such determinations are oftentimes based the subjective impressions of the attorneys. At the time this trial took place, the defense was allotted twice as many strikes as the prosecution.

The *Atlanta Constitution*'s correspondent, reporting on the end of jury selection and the anticipation of the trial testimony beginning the next day, cast high hopes for the Wilcox defense team, referring to Bobby Lee Cook as "Georgia's best criminal defense attorney." As for the district attorney, Lamar Cole, readers were simply reminded that "he [had] lost another well-publicized case" recently, subtly suggesting that perhaps the outcome in this prosecution might be in doubt as well.[83]

Perhaps the most meaningful comment reported in the press, however, came from Quinton "Doc" Griffin, Hellen Hanks's brother. "You hear a lot of people talk about what good, upstanding people the Wilcoxes are, but you don't hear much about how [Hellen] was a good mother, and how her children were left for years not knowing whether their mother had deserted them or what."[84]

Chapter 14

The Trial: Day 3—Sworn Witnesses

With jury selection completed, trial testimony formally began on Wednesday morning, January 6th. The afternoon before, Judge Lilly had announced that the proceedings would be moved to the federal building near the courthouse. Spectators for the jury-selection phase of the trial had been "modest" in number, but on Wednesday, crowds began to gather at 7:00 A.M., two hours in advance of the scheduled start time. A deputy from the Lowndes County Sheriff's Department "turned away 60 to 80 for the opening of court." [85] Judge Lilly instructed that the press and members of the families involved were to be given priority seating in the windowless paneled courtroom over the US Post Office. The *Valdosta Daily Times* reported:

> *As the judge looks out on the courtroom, the rows on his right are occupied primarily by family and friends of Keller Wilcox, the front row usually seating other members of Valdosta's legal establishment. The front row on his left is filled with members of the press, brandishing notebooks, artist's pads, pens, pencils and recording devices. They represent newspapers from Valdosta, Atlanta and Jacksonville, Florida, radio and TV stations from Valdosta, Tallahassee, Florida, and Albany, in addition to Associated Press and United Press International. In the rows behind them are members of the Hanks and Griffin families.*[86]

The jury was seated and sworn. Lilly briefly laid out their obligations. Lamar Cole and Dwight May would be representing the state, and Bobby Lee Cook and Wilby Coleman the defendant. Both sides gave brief opening statements.

Speaking for the prosecution, Cole was confident that the state could prove the "essential elements" of the crime "beyond a reasonable doubt." He asked the jury to pay careful attention to the exact timing of events on the day Hellen Hanks disappeared. The state would offer testimony about what appeared to be conflict between Keller Wilcox and the victim, presumably resulting from his sexual harassment of her. There would be testimony from Ed Wrentz and possibly Lorenzo Marshall (for whom immunity was being considered) about the burial of Hanks's body, as well as other clues found in the grave that spoke to the nature of the crime.

Cook said without hesitation that Keller Wilcox was not guilty "in fact and in absolute good conscience." He spoke at length as to the whereabouts of Keller and Foxy on the day Hellen Hanks disappeared, attempting to establish the fact that they could not have committed the crime. He raised the issue of Hellen Hanks being observed getting into a car with an unknown man on "August 31st" (ignoring evidence that this event took place the day before). He condemned what he described as harsh interrogation by the police of Wrentz and others, implying that the statements made during the interviews were both forced and false. Finally, Cook said that he intended to put both of the Wilcoxes, father and son, on the stand to testify and be cross-examined by the state. He noted that they had been fully cooperative with investigators and had nothing to hide from the jury.

With opening statements completed, witness testimony began. Following standard procedure, witnesses for the state would be heard first, questioned by Cole or May, then cross-examined by Cook or Coleman. The defense would present its witnesses after the prosecution rested its case. James Hanks, Hellen's husband, would be the first witness for the state.

Hanks testified that he had been at work at the Lowndes Correctional Institution from 8:00 A.M. until 4:00 P.M. on the day his wife disappeared. He'd picked up his daughter from school and arrived home about 4:30 P.M. Around 4:55 P.M. he got a call from Keller Wilcox, asking if knew where Hellen was.

Concerned, he immediately drove to Wilcox Advertising, arriving about 5:25 or 5:30. He entered the office to find Keller going through his wife's pocketbook, looking for some keys. Hanks took the pocketbook, and finding an unknown set of keys, handed them back to Keller, who remarked, "She won't be needing these anymore." Two policemen arrived shortly thereafter. Hanks made a brief inspection of the Wilcox office and warehouse before leaving around 6:00 P.M. Other than Keller and the two officers, he saw no one else. Specifically, neither Foxy Wilcox nor his car—a green 1970 Lincoln Continental—were there, according to Hanks. He identified his wife's green dress, reassembled and placed on a dressmaker's dummy, as well as her green beads and her wedding ring. Hellen's dress, a silent if constant reminder of her memory, would remain in the courtroom throughout the trial.

On cross-examination by Cook, Hanks confirmed that Keller made no attempt to stop him from searching the premises. No mention was made of Foxy Wilcox's presence or absence. In response to a direct question, Hanks did note a stake-bodied truck was in the parking lot in addition to his wife's car and the police cruiser.[a]

The state's next witness was Dorothy Ann Edwards, who identified herself as Hellen Hanks's "best friend." She testified about a conversation she'd had with Hellen on Sunday, August 27th, four days before she vanished. Hellen said Keller had "grabbed her at work" "on the bottom" and that she had "turned around and slapped him." She told Dorothy, "I am afraid of him. If you could have seen the look that come on his face. I am afraid of him."

Cora Arduengo, an accountant, was called to the stand following Dorothy Edwards. She had known Hellen both socially and through

---

[a] A "stake-bodied truck" is a work vehicle, generally larger than a pickup, with a flatbed behind the cab that can be enclosed by inserting the stakes of wooden side panels into holes on the sides of the flatbed. Wilcox's stake-bodied truck was described by Willard King as having an approximate twenty-foot-long bed with three-foot-high side panels. The presence of this truck would have significance to be revealed later in the trial.

their children, who'd played together. She recounted a conversation that took place on Tuesday, August 29th, two days before Hellen's disappearance. Both women were at Sandra Williams's beauty shop. Hellen told Cora that she needed to find another job, stating, "I've just got to get away from Wilcox." When asked why she wasn't satisfied working there, Hellen said,

> *"Well, I'll tell you this in confidence. I know you're not going to say anything about it, but I am keeping two sets of books. One is okay, one is not okay. I don't like the position I'm in. I have a lot of trouble with these two sets of books, and I'm scared of the younger Wilcox. I'm scared of the young Wilcox boy."*

Arduengo explained that she didn't report the conversation when Hellen went missing, primarily because the newspapers said "she'd just disappeared and had gone away."

On cross-examination, Cook demanded to know why, as an accountant familiar with IRS rules, she didn't report the allegation of two sets of books to the authorities. Arduengo responded that she "didn't know what the books were."

The state next called Jerry Davis, who at the time served in the military but was working for Wilcox Advertising in August 1972. He testified that "about two weeks before" Hellen's disappearance, he observed "some kind of argument" between Hellen and Keller. Keller had allegedly "bumped into her." In turn, Davis described Hellen as being "highly disturbed." On the day she vanished, Davis was at the Wilcox office between about 8:15 and 8:30 A.M. He was apparently the last person—other than her killer—to see Hellen alive.

At this point, further questioning of Davis by Cole took an unexpected turn. Davis stated that on the afternoon of August 31st, he'd arrived back in Valdosta about 4:00 P.M., going directly to his home. About "five minutes" later, Keller Wilcox and a policeman showed up at his door. Keller questioned him, "conducting an investigation." The police officer said nothing. He also volunteered that "when I left that morning it was a blue car, I can't remember exactly—I believe a

Camaro or a Chevy was setting there with an Alabama license plate." He then testified that after Keller and the policeman left, he went back to the Wilcox office where he "met" Foxy Wilcox and James Hanks. Cole immediately pointed out that his testimony was different from what Davis told the Georgia Bureau of Investigation (GBI) agents when interviewed earlier. "The state is surprised and entrapped by this inconsistency," Cole said.

On cross-examination, Cook had Davis confirm that he had seen "Keller, Mr. Wilcox, Senior, Mr. Hanks and the police," at the office, and that he observed the strange car with the Alabama tag, in the process establishing Foxy Wilcox's whereabouts and reinforcing the presence of the unexplained vehicle on August 31st.

On redirect[b] examination, Lamar Cole questioned Davis about the exact timing of his visit to Wilcox Advertising that afternoon. Davis testified that he arrived there "about 4:20 or 4:30," that James Hanks had questioned him, and that he'd left the office before 5:00 P.M. His statements were at odds with both those of James Hanks and notes from his GBI interview, but seemed to support the defense's emerging narrative.

The state next called John Wesley Goodman, who worked for Wilcox Advertising in 1972. "A few days or weeks" before her disappearance, he observed Hellen "push [Keller's] hand out of the way." "I thought he was feeling on her," Goodman said. He further related that Keller had called her "a dumb bitch," qualifying that by saying, "He

---

[b] By way of clarification for those not familiar with courtroom terminology, the terms "direct examination" and "cross-examination" refer to the questioning of a witness by an attorney. "Direct examination" is the questioning of a witness by the side who called that witness, whereas "cross-examination" refers to the questioning of the same witness by the other side. By way of example, a witness for the prosecution would undergo "direct" questioning from a district attorney and be "cross-examined" by a defense attorney. If the witness is then again questioned by the prosecution, it would be "redirect," or by the defense, "recross," etc.

usually cussed quite a bit, you know, not only her but the rest of the employees, too."

On cross-examination, Goodman admitted that he'd been harshly and aggressively questioned by the police after Hellen's remains were discovered and that he'd been accused of her murder and told that he was lying if he refused to admit it. His interrogators told him his fingerprints were on the cash box found in the grave and suggested that he had raped her before he killed her. Goodman denied it all.

On redirect questioning, Lamar Cole stated that Goodman's testimony, like that of Davis before him, was at odds with what he said earlier to the GBI. "We submit that we're surprised by the difference between what he's now saying and what it's reported that he said to [GBI Agent] Oxford."

Lucy Hanks, Hellen's daughter, was the next to testify. Described by the *Atlanta Constitution*'s correspondent as "a tall, attractive blond woman, [she] was fifteen when her mother vanished. Crying softly, she testified that her mother dropped her off at Lowndes County High on the morning of August 31, 1972, and she never saw her again."[87] Confirming her father's testimony, she identified the green dress on the dressmaker's dummy and the beads as what her mother was wearing on the day of her disappearance. Lucy told of how, several weeks prior, her mother "was very upset when she came home from work one day and she was crying." Lucy continued, "I asked her what was wrong and she said she had to slap [Keller] because he made a pass at her. And she didn't go any further."

"I see," Cole said. "You were fifteen."

"Yes," Lucy replied.

On the evening of August 31, 1972, three police officers responded to the "missing person" call from Wilcox Advertising: Patrolman Gene Allen Deloach, Captain Taylor Davis, and Captain Ransom M. Bass. At the time of the trial, Davis had been dead for about a year. The two remaining officers were called to testify for the state.

Deloach and Davis responded initially to the call from Keller Wilcox. Bass, who acted as a police department investigator, arrived somewhat later. Deloach wasn't sure what time the department had received the call but estimated that he and Davis stayed between thirty minutes and an hour, leaving shortly after Captain Bass arrived. Davis searched the office and warehouse; Deloach did not. In addition to the other officers, he recalled seeing only James Hanks and Keller Wilcox. He did not see Foxy Wilcox.

Ransom Bass, who by 1982 had become Valdosta's assistant police chief, testified that he arrived at Wilcox Advertising after the other officers, between 5:30 and 6:00 P.M. Again, he testified that he saw only Keller Wilcox, James Hanks, and the two other policemen. He did not recall seeing Foxy Wilcox, whom he knew. Bass searched the grounds but not the building, as Davis said he'd already checked it. He stated the stake-bodied truck, the police car, and the cars identified as those of Keller Wilcox and Hellen Hanks were the only vehicles present. Bass estimated that he left at approximately the same time as the other officers, around 6:30 P.M.

To dispel some of the mystery of the strange car with the Alabama tag possibly seen at Wilcox Advertising, Donald M. Wright testified. In August 1972, he was employed at Wilcox's Albany, Georgia, office and was assisting with the management agreement affiliation between the Wilcox and Lamar companies. On August 30th, the day before Hellen Hanks's disappearance, Wright and his secretary drove from Albany to Valdosta, arriving at approximately 10:00 A.M. and staying until about 3:00 P.M. He was driving a brown Chevrolet Malibu with a "fluorescent green" Alabama tag. Around the middle of the day, he and the two women left the office for lunch, staying gone about an hour.

The final witness of the day was Valdosta Chief of Police Allen Loyce Arnold, who in 1972 investigated Hellen Hanks's disappearance in his then-role as assistant chief and "investigative officer" of the city police department. His inquiry began on September 1st and lasted several days. He searched the Wilcox office, warehouse, and grounds and interviewed a number of individuals, including members of Hellen's family. He did not make a formal report of the box found missing on September 9th from the company warehouse and could not recall making the statement that Hellen left with some man. After investigating the mystery vehicle reportedly seen at the Wilcox office, Arnold was satisfied that it was the one driven by Don Wright from Albany. An unsigned report from police files was a summary of notes Arnold had dictated to a department secretary, he said.

Arnold was present at the crime scene investigation when the victim's remains were found in November 1980. It was only then that the case became a criminal investigation. He recalled that Keller was there on the scene and reminded him that he had reported a missing box shortly after Hanks vanished. The box unearthed by the Blantons' plow appeared to be the same or a similar box.

By the time court adjourned for the day, the state appeared to have established through witness testimony that Keller Wilcox had sexually harassed Hellen Hanks, that she was afraid of him, and that she was actively seeking another job. Three witnesses denied seeing Foxy Wilcox at the office on the evening of August 31st. The testimony of another witness, alleging that Foxy was in fact there, was suspect because of conflicts between his cited timeline and that of other witnesses.

Chapter 15

The Trial—Day 4: The State Builds Its Case

The crowds on January 7th, the second day of trial testimony, confirmed the interest in what had become Valdosta's most closely watched criminal case in recent memory. Would-be spectators began gathering at 7:00 A.M., a pattern that would continue throughout the trial. As one reporter described the scene, "Interest in the trial is acute. Robert Carter, sheriff of Lowndes County, stood up in the crowded courtroom Thursday and asked spectators to move their cars from the Pic 'n' Save parking lot, which is across the street from the Federal Building. There was no room for grocery shoppers to park."[88] During the course of the day, the state would call twelve witnesses, continuing to build its case against the defendant.

The first to testify was Fran Lofton, a clerk at the Minit Food Shop on West Hill Avenue, next to Wilcox Advertising. Based on their frequent visits to the convenience store, she said she knew Hellen Hanks and both of the Wilcoxes well but was unable to remember if she had seen Hellen on the day she disappeared, or earlier in the week. Previously, she had told investigators that she recalled seeing Hellen on the morning of August 31st, even describing her green dress and beads. Her loss of memory was unexplained.

Next, GBI investigator Larry Oxford, one of the agents sent to Valdosta in October 1972, said that he was present when Keller Wilcox was interviewed at the local Holiday Inn on the 11th of that month. He testified that Keller reported arriving back in town from Atlanta about 3:45 P.M. on August 31, 1972, and that he and his father—taking separate vehicles—arrived at the Wilcox office about 4:00 P.M. Keller denied to the agents that he'd called Hellen Hanks "a whore or a bitch" or that he had sexually harassed her. On cross-examination, Bobby Lee Cook criticized Oxford for not following up on the report of the vehicle with an Alabama tag allegedly seen at the Wilcox office earlier that same day.

Fred Blanton, who, with his brother Sidney, found Hellen Hanks's remains, was called to the stand and reviewed for the jury the details of the startling discovery. The property where she had been buried was just south of Valdosta, he testified, located on the first dirt road one encountered after the Old Clyattville Road crossed over I-75. His description of picking up "a leg bone" caused an outburst among the courtroom spectators. Judge Lilly warned the crowd that such displays would not be tolerated.

Harry Lynch, who was employed at Chemical Specialties, Inc., a business located "right next door" to Wilcox Advertising, reported seeing nothing "suspicious taking place" at the Wilcox office during the entire week of August 31, 1972.

Mary Alice May, who had worked as the secretary at Wilcox Advertising for five or six months in 1971, testified regarding a lock and key system allowing access to the company's on-site gasoline tank used to fuel the vehicles. The business's secretary, she recalled, was generally in charge of keeping the key. Cook objected to this line of questioning, calling it immaterial and irrelevant. Cole explained,

> *We have already alluded to the fact that possession of the keys and how they were handled is a part of the state's case. We intend to show that certain keys and a lock were found at the burial site of Mrs. Hanks. So we think that who kept the keys, where they were kept, not only the exact day she disappeared, but the course of conduct of doing that during the few months before she disappeared could have a possible bearing on how they were done on that particular day.*

Judge Lilly overruled the objection.

On cross-examination, May said Keller Wilcox was working at the business during her tenure there. In response to Wilby Coleman's question, she said he had always treated her "with kindness and respect."

Arlie Smith, an investigator with the Lowndes County Sheriff's Department in November 1980, was the officer who first responded to the call from the Blanton brothers regarding the discovery of possible human remains off Indian Ford Road. He was also the one who called Keller Wilcox that night after finding documents bearing the name of Wilcox Advertising at the burial site. He described the details of the excavation and processing of the crime scene, which lasted overnight and into the next day. On cross-examination, Wilby Coleman's line of questioning seemed to be pointed at establishing that the techniques used to examine the gravesite could have destroyed important evidence. Smith disagreed.

One of the most important witnesses of the day, Dr. James W. Howard, director of the Moultrie Branch Crime Lab, was next to testify. He arrived at the burial site about 9:00 P.M. on November 24th and actively participated in the excavation of the box and the recovery of evidence. He reviewed for the court items that had been entered as exhibits: a vinyl C&S Bank bag, two metal cash boxes, one of which had been damaged, pieces of green cloth that when reassembled formed the green dress identified as the one Hellen Hanks was wearing on August 31, 1972, a brassiere, a slip, girdle and panties which "had been rolled up and were in a little ball when found," a pair of sandals, a mass of hair, and a forty-six inch-long piece of rope. Both the dress and the brassiere appeared to have been "cut"—presumably off the body—before the corpse was placed in the box.

The length of rope emerged as an object with a possible direct relation to Hanks's death. Five small fragments of hair were found embedded in it. These appeared identical to the "mass of hair" presumed to be the victim's. Cole asked, "Then these hairs that were embedded in this rope, were they consistent with hairs which had been embedded in the rope while the victim was still alive or had not been long dead, and that it remained that way until the body decomposed, the body dropped away from the hair, more or less?"

"That would be consistent with what I found," Dr. Howard replied.

Despite its years inside the buried box, the rope retained an unexplained loop, leading Cole to ask, "Do you have any opinion from your knowledge of fibers as to why it appears to loop like this? Is there anything that makes ropes assume a certain position?"

Howard said, "If the rope had been crossed or tied in some fashion might account for the loops and the bends."

"If it had been left that way over a period of time?" Cole asked.

"Yes."

"Would it be consistent with having been left around something the size of a neck for a period of years."

"Yes, that's possible," Howard answered.

"And then the flesh dropped away and decayed...," Cole began, only to be interrupted by Cook's objection.

On cross-examination, Cook attacked Dr. Howard on the basis of his background education (a doctorate in inorganic chemistry from the University of Virginia), his examination of the evidence found at the crime scene, and his failure to do certain tests (e.g., examine certain pieces of evidence for fingerprints or the presence of blood) that Howard often felt were unnecessary. Cook also pointed out that fiber analysis of the rope found in the buried box was of a different type than sections of rope found at Wilcox Advertising in 1980, more than eight years later.

After a lunch break, court resumed at 2:00 P.M. Eddie Crow, who in November 1980 was a lieutenant with the Lowndes County Sheriff's Department, testified that he took the skull and a partial dental plate found at the Indian Ford Road burial site to Dr. Robert Jackson, who had been Hellen Hanks's dentist. With the chain of custody thus established, Dr. Jackson testified that he could definitively identify the dental work (and hence the skull) as being that of the victim.

Jean Johannessen, Keller Wilcox's ex-wife, was tentatively scheduled as the next witness, which brought up the issue of the defense's unresolved motions *in limine.* The defense sought to bar her from testifying for two reasons: First, the fact that she had been hypnotized might have altered her testimony as a result of false memories suggested by her hypnotist. Second, the defense contended that anything she might say would be considered inadmissible under the doctrine of the confidentiality of marital communications.

With the jury out of the courtroom, both issues were discussed at length. Accepting the state's arguments and based on case law, Judge Lilly ruled that marital privilege did not apply, thus rejecting this as a reason for excluding Johannessen's testimony. To resolve the issue of hypnosis, the defense called Johannessen to testify, followed by Charlie Spray and Billy Selph, two of the officers who had been present when she was questioned and placed under hypnosis.

Jean Johannessen, described by a reporter as "a brown-eyed young woman, with long dark hair,"[89] spoke under oath of her three interviews with investigators, the failed first attempt to hypnotize her, and the second attempt, which was successful. She stated that she had already told the police everything she knew, denying that hypnosis produced any new revelations. Spray and Selph basically confirmed her testimony. The only new fact that seemed to emerge from her trance was the recollection that while driving to the party at Ocean Pond, she'd turned on her windshield wipers because of rain. All parties appeared to agree that "memories" revealed by hypnosis would be inadmissible. Judge Lilly would allow Johannessen to recount only that information she had revealed to investigators prior to her hypnosis session. The motion *in limine* to completely bar her testimony was denied.

As a final issue before testimony resumed, Bobby Lee Cook, speaking for the defendant, stated he had no objection to granting immunity to Lorenzo Marshall, raising the possibility of two witnesses whose testimony could be devastating for his case.

The state called Jean Johannessen back to the stand, this time in the presence of the jury. Having occasionally worked at Wilcox

Advertising during her marriage to Keller, she identified the box that contained Hellen Hanks's remains as being the "same or similar" to a box that was at the warehouse in August 1972. She confirmed the lock and key system that controlled access to the gasoline pump. In regard to company vehicles, she recalled the relatively new 1971 Ford F-100 pickup and that there were two ignition keys, one carried by Keller and a spare key kept at the office.

Shortly after 5:00 P.M. on the afternoon of August 31, 1972, Jean received a call from Keller telling her that Hellen Hanks was missing and that he'd be late for a 7:00 P.M. dinner party given in honor of their recent wedding. Importantly, he told her that he and his father had arrived at the Wilcox office "between three and three-thirty," at least an hour-and-a-half prior to his call. Keller said he'd also notified the police and Hellen's husband.

Johannessen arrived at Ocean Pond shortly before seven o'clock, apologetic that her husband would be late. Keller and his father arrived around nine o'clock. She was certain and testified specifically to the fact that they both came together in the same vehicle, a point that would be challenged in later testimony. She thought it strange that for the first "fifteen or twenty minutes" after his arrival Keller failed to acknowledge her presence, instead speaking with other guests who'd gathered around to hear what had happened to delay them. Dinner was served shortly thereafter, and the party broke up around ten-thirty. Keller said that he needed to go back to the office to check on things; Jean went straight home and was in bed by eleven. In response to a direct question, she said she didn't know whom Wilcox left with. Keller returned home sometime during the night and was there when she awoke the next morning.

During cross-examination, Wilby Coleman asked about what Jean saw that next morning. "I presume that your house wasn't all clogged up with mud tracks and big globs of mud and dirt all over the house, was it?" She replied that it was not. Coleman continued, "You didn't find any mud or thick, heavy wet dirt on Keller's shoes or clothes or anything else, did you?" Jean answered negatively once again.

On redirect examination Dwight May asked Johannessen if Keller did yard work or knew how to use a shovel. She replied, "He knew how to use a shovel, but he wasn't terribly good at it, so I ended up planting most of the bushes." She went on to say that at times Wilcox employees had come out and "dug up shrubbery" for the couple. Cook objected, saying, "It's hard to see how this landscaping has anything to do with this case," calling the line of questioning "immaterial" and "irrelevant." May responded,

> *I think the evidence will show in this case that a certain hole was dug that evening and Mr. Keller Wilcox did not dig the hole but someone else did it for him. And I was simply going to ask this witness whether or not he was accustomed to using a shovel, whether or not he dug in his yard, or got other folks to do it for him.*

Judge Lilly overruled the objection. Jean Johannessen went on to say that Keller used the company's employees as yard help.

The final two witnesses of the day were Martha King and Willard King, Jean Johannessen's parents. Martha testified first. The couple had been at the Ocean Pond party given in honor of Jean and Keller on August 31st. She noted that Foxy and Keller arrived at the same time, observing that "they came up the steps together." She didn't know if they arrived in the same vehicle or separately. She confirmed that the evening was punctuated by scattered rain showers, sometimes heavy. Mrs. King found it unusual that after arriving "Keller didn't go over and greet my daughter in any way," noting they'd only been married for "about twenty-something days" and he had not seen her since earlier in the week.

Willard King had come to work full time for Wilcox Advertising in 1973 and was still working there as production manager in January 1982. During his testimony, he was able to identify the box that contained the victim's remains as being the same or similar to the one he reported missing in 1972. He was quite familiar with the Wilcox company's small fleet of trucks and reported that the "beige" Ford F-100 that Keller often drove in 1972 had been repainted and sold to a man named Salem Scott, who lived in Quitman, Georgia.[a] He recalled that they could only find one ignition key at the time of the sale.

Lamar Cole asked King about the timing of Foxy's and Keller's visit with him in Cordele on the way back from Atlanta on August 31, 1972. They left for home at 1:30 P.M. Given the speed limits and driving times of the day, he estimated they would have arrived in Valdosta around 3:15 P.M. Referring to the fact that James Hanks testified he had been called by Keller about 5:00 P.M., Cole asked, "Through that hour and forty-five minute period, between 3:15 and 5:00, do you know where Foxy Wilcox was, or Keller Wilcox was?" King said he did not.

As it was getting late and it had been a long day in court, Judge Lilly deferred the defense's cross-examination of Willard King until the next morning. He adjourned the day's session. Elements of the state's case were coming into focus: the question of Foxy's and Keller's activities between 3:15 and 5:00 P.M. and again between 6:30 and 9:00 P.M. on the day Hellen Hanks disappeared, Keller's activities after he left the party at Ocean Pond that night, and the as-yet-to-be revealed significance of the beige F-100 pickup and the locking system for the fuel pump.

---

[a] Other witnesses at times referred to this truck as being "yellow" or "tan."

Chapter 16

The Trial—Day 5: A Locksmith and a Deaf-and-Mute Hairdresser

A reporter for the *Atlanta Constitution* wrote of the third day of trial testimony in terms that might have been used to describe the arrival of a traveling circus:

> *A white-haired bailiff was nearly trampled Friday as spectators sought seats in the courtroom. The shopping center across the street has a patrolman to keep out the cars of the curious and ensure parking space for customers. Local radio stations trumpet almost hourly updates as interest continues to grow in the best show in town.*[90]

Willard King, Keller Wilcox's ex-father-in-law, was called back to the stand for cross-examination by the defense. Most of the questioning focused on the physical layout of the Wilcox Advertising office and warehouse, perhaps in an effort to point out to jurors that break-ins were possible and had occurred occasionally.

Salem Franklin Scott, a resident of Quitman, Georgia, was the next witness for the state. In 1979, Scott purchased the beige Ford F-100 pickup that was frequently driven by Keller Wilcox around the time Hellen Hanks disappeared. This was assumed by the prosecution to be the vehicle used to dispose of Hanks's corpse. By the time Scott purchased the truck, it had been painted green by Willard King, then a full-time employee of Wilcox Advertising. Scott testified that he'd received only one ignition key with the truck, a notable fact in light of earlier testimony from Jean Johannessen that there had been two such keys supplied with the vehicle when it was purchased.

Some months after buying the truck, Scott lost his one ignition key. Unable to start the vehicle, he had the ignition lock assembly removed and had a new one—requiring a different key—installed in its place. Later, at Hanks's burial site, several pertinent items were found in the grave. These included a padlock with a key inserted in it, a Ford Motor Company ignition key, and a small key-code tag, the type given out with new vehicle purchases and stamped with a code that would allow a locksmith to cut a new key to fit an ignition. These were discovered "contained in or wrapped up more or less in [a] portion of [the] green dress, and the dress was found under about six inches of dirt beneath the metal-covered box." In trying to decipher the significance of these items, Officer Billy Selph of the LCSD tracked the truck to Salem Scott who, for reasons unknown, had kept the original ignition lock assembly. Selph also visited the Wilcox Advertising office and collected a group of random spare keys the company had on hand.

The state next called William Devoir, a local locksmith with thirty-five years of experience in the business. Devoir examined the padlock and its key. They showed evidence of being buried. When shown a padlock key collected by Selph from the Wilcox office, the locksmith testified that it was a duplicate of the one in the lock—the codes stamped on both keys were the same. The Ford Motor Company key found in the grave fit the original ignition assembly taken from Salem Scott's truck. In a dramatic courtroom demonstration, Cole had Devoir fabricate a new ignition key in front of the jury based on the key-code tag found in the grave. It, too, fit the ignition assembly from what had been Keller Wilcox's truck.

The testimony of Scott and Devoir, in conjunction with the evidence collected from Wilcox Advertising and the burial site, was of vital importance to the state's case. The keys connected the Wilcox office to the burial and supported the theory that the truck used to carry the body to its secret gravesite was driven by Keller Wilcox, who would have had the only other ignition key.

Detective Lieutenant Billy Selph was sworn next. His testimony would take up most of the remainder of the day. On direct examination by Lamar Cole, Selph generally recounted the collection of evidence from the burial site, including the discovery of the lock and keys. He noted that the looped section of rope found in the box with the bones was of the "general shape and size" of those found in a "lard can" in the paper room at the Wilcox Advertising office when it was searched in 1980. He also identified "a photograph of a pair of cutting shears or a pair of scissors that was kept in the paper room on a shelf underneath [a] table," about four feet from the bucket of ropes.

In response to accusations that investigators' search for suspects was racially motivated and aimed primarily at blacks, Selph denied this, pointing out that with the exception of Hellen Hanks and the Wilcoxes, all of the employees at Wilcox Advertising's Valdosta office were African American. Anyone who worked there was a potential suspect.

Selph recounted a conversation that he had with Keller Wilcox not long after Hanks's remains were discovered. The investigation was just getting started; Ed Wrentz had not yet given a statement to investigators. Selph said he was at the Wilcox office,

> *"drawing a floorplan of the building, measuring it and drawing it. Myself and Sergeant Spray and I believe Keller, I believe we were the only ones in the office, we were sitting in Keller's office. He asked me what I thought about the disappearance of Mrs. Hanks, if I thought somebody had come in and kidnapped her and taken her out to the location in the woods somewhere and possibly killed her and then come back and stole the box and took it out there and buried her. And I told him no, that I didn't think that. That I thought she was killed in the building, and put in that box and then transferred out there."*

Lamar Cole asked, "And how did he respond to that?"

"He didn't say anything," Selph replied.

On cross-examination, Bobby Lee Cook brutally and relentlessly attacked Selph, questioning and condemning his handling of evidence, his documentation of it, and the investigation in general. He berated him for not doing enough to find the couple across the street who reported seeing the car with the Alabama tags around the time Hellen Hanks vanished. Cook condemned the way in which Selph and

Captain Billy Register interrogated potential suspects, essentially all of whom were African American. Reading from transcripts of the interrogations, Cook quoted the officers threatening to "fry your ass" to one suspect and falsely suggesting that his fingerprints were on evidence recovered from the gravesite. They suggested another suspect might be lynched and accused another of lying, saying, "God's going to strike you dead."

In response to Cook's seeming outrage over the intensive questioning, Selph defended the officers' actions, stating, "We had a murder case that we were investigating. The purpose of a legal investigation in a murder case is to obtain all the facts and seek out the truth. We had a woman who was murdered, who left a family of husband and children. And I would do it all over again."

On redirect examination, Cole elicited an important fragment of testimony from Selph, something that led them to take a special interest in Ed Wrentz. On their initial interview with Wrentz, "he advised us that he was a retired employee, that he was not working at that particular time," Selph said. But when investigators obtained the employment records seeking the names of possible suspects, "I noted that he was drawing what appeared to be a full-time weekly paycheck."

Dr. Park Dietz, author of the letter suggesting that evidence found at the scene of Hellen Hanks's burial indicated a sex crime, was scheduled as the state's next witness. But there were potential problems with his testimony, problems acknowledged by both the prosecution and defense. To resolve these issues, Dr. Dietz and attorneys for both sides met in the judge's chambers for a brief hearing away from the jury. The issue was Dr. Dietz's report, which had been delivered to investigators and the prosecution team in September 1981. In November 1981, two months before the start of the trial, the Georgia Supreme Court issued an opinion in an unrelated case as to the timing of when evidence, including scientific reports, had to be made available to a defendant's lawyers.[a] Dietz's report, strongly supporting the contention that Hellen Hanks's murder should be classed as a sex crime, had not been made available to Keller Wilcox's lawyers in a timely manner as prescribed by law. Despite his reservations, Cole was forced to agree with Judge Lilly, who pointed out that putting Dietz on the stand would provide clear grounds for reversal of a guilty verdict. Lilly affirmed the defense's motion to suppress Dietz's testimony, dealing a harsh blow to the state's case.

Sandra Williams was Hellen Hanks's hairdresser, and would be able to testify regarding a conversation she'd had with her a few days before Hellen's disappearance. There was one problem, however: Sandra Williams had been deaf and mute since birth. She "listened" by lipreading and "spoke" via sign language, formidable barriers to communication before a jury in a court of law. In order for Williams to testify, the state brought in Charlene Lavine, an employee of the Georgia Department of Human Resources and certified as an interpreter by the National Registry of Interpreters for the Deaf. Lavine proposed to communicate with the witness by a combination of lipreading and sign language.

In establishing Lavine's qualifications as a lip-reader, she reported that "between sixty and seventy percent of what is said on the mouth looks like something else." The defense promptly took this to mean that lipreading was only thirty to forty percent accurate, an assertion denied by the interpreter. Bobby Lee Cook objected to her testimony, alleging "anything that the interpreter would relate that she had read the [on the] lips of Mrs. Hanks would be the subject matter of speculation, conjecture and hypothesis and would not have the degree of reliability which the law would require. And we, therefore, say that such testimony would be incompetent as a matter of law."

---

[a] *Tanner v. State*, 160 Ga. App. 266 (1981).

In rebuttal, Lamar Cole pointed out that witnesses who wore glasses or were even blind in one eye were qualified to testify as to what they might have seen. More importantly, Cole pointed out, "There's a statute which specifically states that a person shall not be disqualified as a matter of law because of impaired ability." Judge Lilly ruled that Sandra Williams—via Charlene Lavine—was competent to testify.

Sandra Williams had known Hellen Hanks since she was "a little girl." "We grew up together," she stated. Confirming the testimony of Cora Arduengo, Williams recounted the details of a conversation that took place at her beauty salon on August 29, 1972. Through the interpreter, she related to the district attorney that Hellen was "scared to death of the young Wilcox boy," that she'd been crying, and "acted upset." Williams also confirmed that Hellen "was talking to Cora something about two sets of books."

The state's final witness for the day was Van Hastings, a patrolman with the Valdosta Police Department (VPD). He was in the front passenger's seat of the patrol car that took Keller Wilcox to the Lowndes County jail after his arrest on the morning of July 3, 1981. During the ride, Hastings testified that Keller voluntarily made two strange statements to the patrolman, whom he knew. In the first, Hastings testified Keller said, "I tried to work with them on this thing. [Keller] said I was in Albany when I heard about the Hanks woman." In the second, Keller admitted to being at the police department a few days before his arrest and overhearing investigators questioning a suspect about the case. He then said, "I'm not going to admit anything until I see some facts."

Before the court adjourned for the weekend, Bobby Lee Cook made a motion to "exclude and strike" the testimony of Sandra Williams, citing possible violations of the Fourth and Fifth Amendments of the Bill of Rights. Lilly refused to grant it, allowing her testimony to stand.

The trial would recess for the weekend, resuming with additional witnesses for the prosecution on Monday, January 11th, leaving the jury with much to ponder. Evidence appeared to link Wilcox Advertising—and implicitly one of its employees—to Hellen Hanks's death and the attempt to hide her body. There was unrefuted testimony that Keller Wilcox had sexually harassed the victim and that she had voiced to others her fear of him. There were emerging discrepancies in the timing of events and the whereabouts of Keller and Foxy Wilcox on the afternoon and evening of August 31, 1972. But the defense had struck blows for its side as well. The testimony of Dr. Park Dietz, important to the state's presumed motive for Hellen's murder, had been suppressed. Bobby Lee Cook's indignation at intimidation tactics used against potential suspects by investigators cast doubt on the state's planned testimony from Ed Wrentz and Lorenzo Marshall. Pundits were not yet publicly making predictions as to outcome, but by the end of the first week neither side appeared to have gained an obvious advantage.

Chapter 17

The Trial—Day 6: The State's Big Witnesses

The weather, which had been reasonably balmy for the first five days of the trial, turned chilly over the weekend. Monday, January 11th, was clear and cold, with temperatures plunging into the teens. The thermometer would scarcely rise above freezing for the first two days of the week. As before, the wooden benches of the courtroom were packed with two sharply divided groups: friends, relatives, and supporters of the defendant on the judge's right, and those of the victim on the judge's left. With the colder weather, one person who attended the trial described the scene as "mink and silk" on one side, and "flannel and denim" on the other.

Those who had read the morning edition of the *Daily Times* were not likely to have missed an editorial by Wink DeVane heaping gentle praise on Bobby Lee Cook.[91] Using words that might usually be reserved for a visiting movie star, DeVane averred that, "Cook's reputation as one of the top trial lawyers in the United States is well deserved. You don't talk about such things in polite conversation, but rumor has it that his fee starts at six figures and goes from there. He's worth it." By way of verification, he noted that two rows of the courtroom benches were packed with lawyers "going to school off Bobby Lee Cook." Remarking tangentially that Lamar Cole had "hung tough" in his confrontations with the famed defense attorney, DeVane summarized his thoughts by saying, "It's been a pleasure to have Bobby Lee Cook in our town. But it will never be the same after this trial is over. He's that good."

If observers such as Wink DeVane were to be believed, the prosecution was down but not out. Cole had chosen to save his most important witnesses, Ed Wrentz and Lorenzo Marshall, for last. Their testimony was critical. If the jury chose to believe it, at least as it was presented at the committal hearing nearly six months earlier, the conviction of Keller Wilcox on a charge of murder would seem almost certain. But as would soon be demonstrated in court, things can change as time goes by, even sworn testimony...

Cole called Lorenzo Marshall as his first witness of the day. Ed Wrentz had implicated Marshall as being the man who helped him bury the box containing Hellen Hanks's body. When questioned in early July 1981, Marshall gave a sworn statement that confirmed the essential elements of Wrentz's admissions to investigators: at the direction of Keller and Foxy Wilcox, he and Wrentz dug a hole and buried a dismembered body identified as the victim.

Marshall was seventy years old, had a fourth-grade education, and by 1972 had been an employee of Wilcox Advertising for twenty years. Within minutes of beginning his testimony, Marshall denied assisting Wrentz in burying a box, stating without hesitation he was in Albany from Tuesday, August 29, through Friday, September 1, 1972. He admitted to signing the statement after interrogation by the police but said he did so under pressure. Marshall's attorney, Cam Hickman, was aware that the witness was "likely" to recant his statement, even though he had been offered full immunity from further prosecution. Hickman admitted to the court, however, that he did not establish whether or not Marshall was recanting *every* single thing he said in his "confession," or only parts of it. That gave Cole the opportunity to cross-examine Marshall as a hostile witness.

On the stand, Marshall freely acknowledged that he had been advised of his rights and signed the statement with that in mind. He confirmed that he had said to investigators essentially everything contained in the document but was now contending that it was not true. Lamar Cole asked, "What's the need in saying it if it's not true?"

"Well," Marshall replied, "they just had me overpowered with words." When asked about the very specific nature of the details in his statement, he replied that the information had come from Ed Wrentz or the police. "I just weakened and couldn't help myself," he explained.

Cole scored a point in discrediting Marshall's changed testimony by asking him which company vehicle he was driving while in Albany. The "stake-body," he replied.[a] When questioned about the possibility of the truck being back in Valdosta on Thursday, the day Hanks disappeared, Marshall replied, "I know we had the truck over in Albany. I drove it back Friday. It did not come back." Other witnesses had testified that the truck was at Wilcox Advertising on Thursday evening, August 31st.

Cole scored again when questioning why Marshall was so sure of the details of his activities during a certain single week nearly a decade earlier when he couldn't seem to remember the details of the week prior. Cole asked, "Well, what about the week before that, where did you work on Monday?"

"I can't remember," Marshall replied."

"You can't? Well, why not?" Cole asked.

"Nobody been refreshing my memory to it," Marshall replied, suggesting that his answers had been coached.

This exchange brought a gale of laughter from the spectators, leading Judge Lilly to reprimand the crowd, stating, "This is not a place of amusement. There's not anything funny about this case. I don't expect to have any demonstrations of amusement; nothing being shown here is for the purpose of amusing anybody." He directed the sheriff to "see to it that this rule is strictly complied with."

On cross-examination, Bobby Lee Cook brought up the name of Ellis Rountree, who was scheduled to testify later as a witness for the defense. Marshall alleged Rountree had been in Albany with him during the week Hellen Hanks disappeared and would be able to confirm his alibi. The remainder of Cook's examination centered on Marshall's interrogation by investigators on July 2, 1981. Reading from the

---

[a] The court reporter transcribed "state body" here and elsewhere, but the reference is clear. This is assumed to be a typographical error when translating oral dialogue into the written word. See footnote on page 76.

transcript of a tape recording, Cook focused on the officers' refusals to believe Marshall's initial denials and the implied threats to his well-being should he not "tell the truth." In the end, Marshall implied his so-called confession was based on pressure from his interrogators.

Following the uncertain testimony of Lorenzo Marshall, Cole called his star witness, Ed Wrentz. Wrentz's testimony was vital to the state but also risky based on the confused statements he made at the committal hearing the previous July. Initially things went well, extremely well. In response to simple and direct questions posed by the district attorney, Wrentz gave simple and direct answers, repeating his previous statements, but with greater deliberation and clarity. He admitted that he and Marshall dug a hole at the direction of Keller and Foxy Wilcox; that they were taken to the site in a pickup truck driven by Keller; that they were interrupted in their digging by rain; that they put a body ("Mrs. Hanks") in a box, noting, "It was stiff," et cetera.

On Cook's cross-examination, however, Wrentz's well-defined narrative fell apart. Appearing at times confused by the defense attorney's badgering and leading questions, Wrentz denied much of what he'd just admitted only minutes before.[b] Cook suggested that many of Wrentz's previous statements were influenced by threats and consisted of information suggested by investigators. Wrentz now had found an alibi. He said he was working in Lake City and Live Oak, Florida, two cities an hour or more south of Valdosta, and that he didn't return to town until Saturday, September 2nd. In the process of his cross-examination, Cook appeared to accidentally introduce information that supported the state's case. Wrentz had told investigators that he read "in the paper" that Hellen Hanks's legs had been cut off prior to her burial. There was a problem with this statement; this information was something the investigators themselves didn't know at the time, and it

[b] A typical exchange: Cook: "And when you told them that you didn't know anything about Mrs. Hanks's disappearance, that was the truth, wasn't it, Mr. Wrentz?" Wrentz: "Yes, sir, that was the truth."

did not appear in the press. If true, this had to be information known only to someone who participated in the burial.[c]

On redirect questioning by Lamar Cole, Wrentz confirmed many of the things he had told the district attorney during his initial questioning earlier in the session, making his testimony even more inconsistent. It seemed evident that his erratic account was in part influenced by his age and fading memory.

Both Marshall and Wrentz, confessed parties to the crime (if their earlier statements could be believed) and able to testify freely under grants of immunity, had given less-than-stellar performances as the state's star witnesses. Depending on how one chose to interpret their statements, they either actively participated in Hellen Hanks's burial or were themselves victims of overzealous investigators and a district attorney eager to get a conviction in this high-profile case. It would be up to the jury to interpret their confusing and contradictory testimony.

To confirm for the jury the contention that Hellen Hanks's legs had been severed prior to her body being placed in the box, the state called Dr. Larry Howard, director of the State Crime Laboratory in Atlanta. Dr. Howard's credentials were solid: he had been engaged in criminal forensics for twenty-five years and director of the crime lab for a decade. He held a doctoral degree in pharmacology and had done post-doctoral work in forensic pathology at Emory University under the previous director of the crime lab. Over his career, Howard had performed some 7,000 autopsies and examined "about fifty skeletons."

Dr. Howard had personally examined Hellen Hanks's remains on two occasions, the first shortly after they were found in late 1980, and again after they were re-exhumed in August 1981 for the specific purpose of searching for evidence of dismemberment. As this detail had not been known prior to Ed Wrentz's confession, neither investigators nor the crime lab initially focused on it. He confirmed that Hellen

---

[c] Wrentz told investigators during the interview that "Mr. Wilcox," i.e., Foxy, cut the legs off.

stood an estimated five feet, nine inches in height, nearly half again longer than the box in which her remains were found. On specific examination, he did find evidence that her legs had been severed at the knees: "two linear abrasions on the back of the left kneecap that had been made by a pointed instrument" and a similar lesion on the femur at the knee joint.[d] When asked to define "linear abrasion," he described this as "something that would be made by a sharp point being dragged across the surface." This was "consistent with a knife blade" and suggested that the lower legs had been removed by cutting from the back of the leg toward the front. He made photographs and took the bones to Maryland to consult with Dr. Ellis Kerley, one of the nation's leading forensic anthropologists. Dr. Kerley agreed with Dr. Howard's conclusions.

When shown the piece of curled rope found in the burial box, Dr. Howard expressed his opinion that Hellen Hanks's death resulted from strangulation, presumably by this rope. The presence of hair tangled in the rope "would be an indication that this cord was originally around the neck." In reference to the cutting of her clothing, he averred, "These two findings I think reinforce each other because many times strangulation of a female victim is associated with sexual assault and that is [the] cause of death in...many of the sexual assault cases."

Cole questioned Dr. Howard regarding the issue of rigor mortis.[e] Howard estimated an average time of onset as four to eight hours after death, but the process could occur sooner, for example, in warmer

---

[d] The femur is the long bone of the leg connecting the hip joint to the knee. Later trial testimony seems to suggest that the right patella ("kneecap") was among the bones missing following the initial excavation at the Indian Ford Road burial site.

[e] "Rigor mortis" (Latin: "stiffness of death"): Rigor mortis is the stiffening of the body that occurs after death, causing difficulty in bending the joints. Its onset is variable based on many factors; an average might be four to eight hours. Rigor can persist for as long as one to three days, with the timing again dependent on a number of factors.

weather or if there had been a struggle or fight immediately preceding death. Regarding the victim's dismemberment, Howard said, "It's hard, very difficult to move the limbs when rigor mortis has occurred. And, of course, these are the circumstances under which a body might have to be cut to fit in a container."

The state's next witness was Dr. Ellis R. Kerley, a nationally known expert in the field of forensic anthropology. Kerley's credentials were impressive: professor at the University of Maryland, past president of the American Board of Forensic Anthropology, and former vice president of the American Academy of Forensic Sciences. In August 1981, he met with Dr. Howard and examined photographs and the bones from Hellen Hanks's legs. He agreed with Howard's conclusion that the left knee joint displayed evidence "consistent with dismemberment."

Notwithstanding Dr. Kerley's credentials, on cross-examination Bobby Lee Cook attempted to introduce an element of doubt by pointing out that Kerley was giving his opinion, and could not say "with absolute certainty...that there was any dismemberment in this case." Kerley agreed.

Cook then turned to the professor's credentials, first establishing that he was not a medical doctor, but instead an anthropologist. Perhaps hoping to appeal to the jurors' religious beliefs, Cook asked, "In the field of anthropology, do you deal with the theory of evolution?"

"Yes," Kerley replied.

"And of Darwin's theory of evolution, the Darwinian theory of evolution?"

"Among others, yes," was the reply.

"That we all evolved from a lower form of life?" Cook continued.

"From an earlier form of life...," Kerley started.

"That we come from monkeys or rodents or what have you...," Cook said, talking over the witness.

"...no," Kerley finished his reply.

The exchange ended on an objection from Lamar Cole as to the relevance of the questioning. Cook explained to the judge that he was "voir diring him [*sic*] in his field of physical anthropology" before moving on to more direct questions.

The final witness of the day was Carl Judge, an air traffic control specialist at the Valdosta Municipal Airport, located approximately a mile to the east of the burial site off Indian Ford Road. Judge was working on the day Hellen Hanks disappeared. Among his duties was the collection of weather data on an hourly basis, including cloud coverage, visibility, shower activity, and the like. These data were held locally for some days before being mailed to an archive facility in Asheville, North Carolina.

Judge was shown a certified copy of local weather records from August 31, 1972. At approximately 7:00 P.M. on that day, there was a report of "rain showers of unknown intensity north through northwest of the airport." As the report was a snapshot of the weather at a certain moment in time, there was no indication as to the intensity of the rain, when it began, or how long it lasted. At the time of the next reading, approximately 8:00 P.M., there were no reports of rain. Ed Wrentz had testified that the first attempt to dig a hole to bury Hellen Hanks's body had been rained out. While Judge's testimony did not exactly correlate with any known timeline, it did document that there had been rain in the general area around the time investigators believed the first attempt at the burial took place. When—again, according to Wrentz—he, Marshall, and the Wilcoxes returned to finish digging the hole, they were not interrupted by rain. The weather records, Judge testified, recorded no signs of precipitation between 6:00 and 8:00 P.M. on the evenings of September 1st and 2nd.

The case against Keller Wilcox was based on bits and pieces of evidence and opinion, a circumstantial jigsaw puzzle that the prosecution hoped the jury would be able to assemble into a conviction. During four days of testimony, the state had presented its witnesses and its experts. But the defense fought back ferociously, doing its best to discredit the police, the prosecutors, and the investigation in general. As one reporter who closely followed the trial would comment later, at this point in the trial, the defense seemed to have the advantage in the case.[92] Moreover, Bobby Lee Cook and the defense team had yet to present their witnesses and experts. The final outcome was far from certain.

Chapter 18

The Trial—Day 7: Foxy Testifies

On Tuesday morning, January 12th, the state formally rested its case. In response, the defense attempted to mitigate damage the state's witnesses might have done to their client's case. Outside of the presence of the jury, Bobby Lee Cook made several motions that, if granted by the judge, would accomplish this end.

First, Cook moved to strike and exclude that portion of Dr. Larry Howard's testimony in which he expressed his opinions that Hellen Hanks's death was caused by strangulation and related to a sexual assault. Disparaging the lab director's credentials, he said, "Such a statement and an opinion, all made by a professed expert with a degree in pharmacology and biochemistry, is a bare and naked conclusion of the declarant which is not based on a sufficient factual predicate as to reasonably or reliably support such a conclusion. It could be no more than bare conjecture and speculation," Cook alleged.

In response, Lamar Cole noted "that an expert may express his opinion but the jury is not bound by his opinion." Judge Lilly denied Cook's motion.

Next, Cook moved to "strike and exclude all of the testimony of Ed Wrentz and request that the court adjudicate after having heard the testimony in this case that he is incompetent as a witness since his testimony and interrogation are under the uncontradicted evidence in this case, a result of the severe, illegal, improper and uncivilized tactics which offend the common standards of decency and norms of Anglo-Saxon law." Here the defense attorney was referring to Wrentz's questioning by investigators.

In response to this motion, Cole asserted that the proper time to question Wrentz's competence would have been at the time of his testimony, noting again that the jury was capable of deciding on the witness's veracity and competency. No mention was made of the fact that Wrentz's testimony, if accepted by the jury, was highly damaging to the defense's case. Cook's motion was denied.

Cook's third major motion asked the court to grant a directed verdict of not guilty on both counts with which Keller Wilcox was charged. He proposed that "the state has failed to carry the burden of proof and failing to prove beyond a reasonable doubt and to a moral and reasonable certainty of the essential allegations as alleged and set forth in both counts of the indictment." "There is no evidence before this court that this defendant either directly or indirectly caused the death in the murder indictment of Hellen Griffin Hanks," Cook declared.

Judge Lilly heard arguments from both sides, including Lamar Cole's, "To be plain-spoken, Judge, there's no way she could have nailed herself into that box either after an accident or a suicide." The motion was denied. Lilly directed the defense to call its first witness, thus beginning the second portion of the trial.

Foxy Wilcox took the stand and was sworn. Under Cook's questioning, he recounted the events of the week Hellen Hanks went missing, beginning with his and Keller's business trip to Atlanta on the 29th, their return on the 31st, and the subsequent investigation. While his general account matched that of other witnesses, there were important differences. On August 31st, Foxy testified that he and Keller left Cordele at about 2:00 P.M., arrived at the north Valdosta I-75 exit ramp at about 4:00 P.M., and at the Wilcox Advertising office about 4:30 P.M. Around 5:00 P.M. they called the police. James Hanks and two policemen arrived at nearly the same time, around 5:20 P.M., he estimated.

Cook asked how long the policemen stayed. "It's my—to the best of my recollection, we all walked out of there, the two policemen, Mr. Hanks, Keller and I walked out approximately just before eight o'clock."

Cook then asked, "Now, did anyone else come there, any other policeman come there during that period of time and on this occasion that you can recall?"

"Not on August 31st, the Thursday, no, sir," was Foxy's answer.

In a clear effort to establish an alibi for Keller, he testified, "From the time we got up that morning until we parted after closing the office, Keller wasn't out of my sight five minutes the entire day."

Foxy Wilcox's testimony in response to Cook's questions was in sharp contrast to the testimony of other witnesses. Willard King had testified that Foxy and Keller left Cordele about 1:30 P.M. and could easily have arrived in Valdosta by 3:15 P.M. There were three members of the Valdosta Police Department who responded to the call of a missing person, not two, as Foxy testified. Importantly, there was previous testimony that James Hanks and all three of the policemen left by around 6:30 P.M., not 8:00. Neither James Hanks nor two of the policemen recalled seeing Foxy Wilcox or his green Lincoln Continental.[a]

Jean Johannessen had testified earlier that Foxy and Keller arrived at the Ocean Pond party in the same vehicle about 9:00 P.M. When asked by Cook how he got to the event, Foxy gave conflicting testimony that he came in a separate car with his wife, his sister-in-law Lota Wilcox, and his aunt and uncle, Mr. and Mrs. Garrard Harrell, arriving "between eight-thirty and nine o'clock."

Foxy's testimony in response to direct questioning by Bobby Lee Cook had gone smoothly. Under cross-examination by Lamar Cole, the atmosphere changed. As Wilcox's testimony was at odds with the series of events postulated by the prosecution, he appeared to resent the district attorney's intensive questioning. Several observers who attended the trial described his attitude as arrogant.

Cole made several important points. Bobby Lee Cook had alleged that investigators targeted African Americans as suspects in Hellen

---

[a] One of the three policemen who responded to the missing person report on the night of August 31, 1972, was deceased at the time of the trial.

Hanks's murder, accusing the police of a racial "round-up." Cole asked, "So, if they wanted to talk to each and every one of your employees, since you worked only black employees, it's only black employees they could talk to, is that right?" Foxy admitted that except for himself, Keller, and Hellen, all of the employees at his Valdosta office were black. The questioning of the possible suspects was not racially motivated.

Foxy again alleged the police had been present from "approximately five-twenty until nearly eight o'clock" and insisted that his 1970 green Lincoln Continental was sitting in the parking lot when the police and James Hanks were there, even though other witnesses denied seeing it. He acknowledged that Keller at times drove "the little tan-colored pick-up truck."

When asked whether he recalled Captain Ransom Bass, the third police officer that responded on August 31st to the missing person call, Foxy said "he came in for a short while," contradicting statements he'd made earlier to Bobby Lee Cook. Foxy said he had no idea why neither the police nor James Hanks recalled seeing him at the office. He vigorously denied that the stake-body truck was present in the Wilcox office parking lot, in contrast to other witnesses who saw it there.

Foxy denied that Keller was searching through Hellen Hanks's purse when James Hanks arrived but did acknowledge that part of her job included keeping the keys to the gas pump, among other things. He admitted that shortly after Hellen disappeared, the lock on the gas pump was discovered to be missing as well, offering various explanations about how that might have happened.

As Lamar Cole began to question Foxy regarding his son's temperament, Bobby Lee Cook requested a conference with the judge. The jury was sent out of the courtroom, at which time Cook moved for a mistrial

> *for the specific reason that the district attorney has intentionally and callously injected into the trial of this case by his cross-examination of Mr. Wilcox, Sr., the witness now on the stand, alleged behavior of the*

defendant concerning serious temper tantrums concerning grabbing somebody by the neck and shaking them. An incident wholly unrelated to any transaction on trial in this case could not be offered for any purpose other than for its prejudicial impact.

When asked by the judge for his response, Cole replied that he was asking about the defendant's temperament, not his character, noting that Foxy had already replied "that [Keller] has no temper, he only hugs people." Judge Lilly denied the motion for a mistrial, but at Cook's request called the jury back and instructed them to ignore answers to any questions posed about the defendant's temperament.

In further questioning, Cole established that in 1972, Foxy's vision, and hence his driving, was limited by cataracts. "I did not drive during the night," he stated. He had earlier said the police and James Hanks did not leave Wilcox Advertising until about 8:00 P.M. on August 31st, after which he and Keller drove separately to their respective houses. The sun set that day at 7:57 P.M.

Continuing his cross-examination, Cole made two final points. As related to who might have dug the hole to bury Hellen's body, Cole got Foxy to admit, "I'm opposed to physical work." In regard to Keller's statement to his wife and investigators that he'd left the Ocean Pond party to check on things at the office, Foxy said, "We locked it up as soon as the police and Mr. Hanks left." No explanation for Keller's return there was offered.

As it was noon, the court adjourned for lunch. Even before the day's testimony was over, however, the afternoon edition of the *Valdosta Daily Times* featured an update on Foxy's courtroom interrogation under the bold headline of "Wilcox's Father Offers Conflicting Testimony." Obviously following the trial proceedings closely, the *Times*'s reporter pointed out the discrepancies in Foxy's version of events as compared to that of other witnesses.[93] Delivered without editorial comment, the news article suggested a possible turn in the direction of the trial.

The defense's next witness was Dr. Joseph L. Burton, a licensed physician and at the time medical examiner for DeKalb and Cobb counties in the metropolitan Atlanta area. Dr. Burton was well qualified. In addition to being a board-certified pathologist, he'd done post-doctoral training in forensic pathology and had formerly served as deputy medical examiner in Dade County (Miami), Florida. During his career, Burton reported that he'd conducted more than 7,000 autopsies. In October 1981 he had traveled to Valdosta to observe the second exhumation of Hellen Hanks's remains. The following month, he examined her bones and took numerous photographs of them at the Georgia State Crime Lab in Atlanta in the presence of Dr. Larry Howard, who had testified for the state earlier in the trial.

In a lengthy and detailed presentation to the jury, Dr. Burton acknowledged seeing several small marks on the bones of the victim's left knee but stated he did not believe these to be definitive evidence of dismemberment. He also stated that, based on his examination, he could not express an opinion as to the exact cause of Hellen Hanks's death.

Dr. Burton had also examined other evidence recovered from the gravesite. On cross-examination he reluctantly admitted to Lamar Cole that the cutting of the victim's clothes was "certainly not inconsistent" with a sex crime but refused to label it as such. He also refused to render an opinion about the rope found in the box which the state's expert thought could have been used to strangle Hanks.

Cole struck a blow to Burton's credibility when he questioned him about a previous case from Clayton County, Georgia, involving a man who died when his Volkswagen was reportedly struck by a train. Burton signed the death certificate even though he never saw the victim's body and had not personally done the autopsy. Based on later information, the man's body was exhumed. It was discovered that he had died from a gunshot wound to the head. Burton readily admitted the error, blaming it on erroneous information given to the physician doing the autopsy.

Following Dr. Burton, Dr. G. J. Austin was called to the stand. Dr. Austin was a pediatrician in Valdosta and attended Keller Wilcox shortly after his birth. He and his wife were Keller's godparents, and cohosts of the party at Ocean Pond on August 31, 1972. He recalled that Foxy was "a little late" in arriving at the party (which started at 7:00 P.M.), further specifying that "my best recollection is that he was, perhaps, forty minutes late." This conflicted with Foxy's own testimony in which he said he didn't leave the Wilcox office until about 8:00, and that of Jean Johannessen who said he arrived at Ocean Pond about 9:00 P.M.

Next, Kevin Riley, president of Lamar Advertising Company, testified briefly about meeting Foxy and Keller in Atlanta in August 1972 and the management agreement between his company and the Wilcoxes. The main point gleaned from his testimony was that during the transition period from manual to computer-based bookkeeping, Wilcox Advertising was keeping both the old and new systems in place until all parties were familiar with the new system. His testimony appeared designed to address the issue of "two sets of books" Hellen Hanks discussed with Cora Arduengo only days prior to her disappearance.

John Wyatt Yow Jr., known familiarly as "Buddy," was the next witness. He was Keller Wilcox's first cousin and one of his "best friends." Wilby Coleman, examining him for the defense, established early in his testimony that Yow suffered from "a physical nervous condition" that was not further defined. Yow stated that on August 31, 1972, he'd decided to pay a spur-of-the-moment visit during his lunch hour to his cousin, Keller, at the Wilcox office. Arriving at about 1:40 P.M., he found the door unlocked, with no one there. After calling out for Keller and getting no response, he went back to his job at Sears & Roebuck.

After leaving work, Yow testified that he decided to go back to the Wilcox office, arriving this time about 6:10 P.M. He stated he saw Keller, his uncle Foxy, and the police there. When he spoke to his uncle, telling him that he'd come by earlier and found the office empty and unlocked, Foxy yelled at him, saying, "Why the hell didn't you call your Aunt Russell?"[b] Yow said he'd remembered these events because his uncle had yelled at him and used profanity. It was the first time he had ever heard him do so.

Yow had testified to Coleman that the Wilcox office was "normally locked between one and two," admitting he'd known that since his childhood. On cross-examination Lamar Cole asked, somewhat skeptically, "Out of all the times [the office] has been locked up since you were a child between one and two, on this one day that Keller needs an alibi you went down there without even telephoning to see if it was locked up?"

"I did," Yow answered.

Cole established that Yow's memory around the time of Hellen Hanks's disappearance was vague. He wasn't sure he remembered the party at Ocean Pond and couldn't remember if he went to it. During the hearings prior to the trial, however, he had contacted Wilby Coleman with his story. This happened after Keller approached him asking if he remembered the events of the day, including the Ocean Pond party, which Yow apparently attended. Cole asked why his memory was so clear as to the "spontaneous ten minutes in the middle of the day" when he couldn't remember other details. Yow replied that it stuck in his mind because it was "the day that Uncle Foxy fussed at me."

"And you remembered that just here lately when Keller refreshed your memory?" Cole asked.

"That's correct," Yow replied.

Next to testify was Daisy Harrell, Foxy Wilcox's aunt and Keller's great-aunt. She vouched for Foxy's testimony that he had ridden with

---

[b] Russell Plowden Wilcox was Foxy's wife, Keller's mother, and Buddy Yow's aunt.

her and three other relatives to the Ocean Pond party on August 31st. She could not remember the exact time they arrived or left.

The defense's next two witnesses were Ellis Rountree and Ed Smith. Both were placed on the stand to verify Lorenzo Marshall's alibi that he was in Albany on August 31st and did not return until the following afternoon. Rountree was first to testify. He stated that he was in Albany with Lorenzo Marshall "the whole week" and that he and several other workers slept in a warehouse in Albany on the night of August 31st. The group returned to Valdosta "around five" on the afternoon of September 1st.

On cross-examination Rountree confirmed that they were riding in the stake-bodied truck, which he said Lorenzo parked at the Wilcox office on their return. He confirmed that police questioned him after Hellen Hanks's body was discovered but said he was not mistreated or intimidated. Importantly, Rountree confirmed that he had talked to Doug Moss, Bobby Lee Cook's investigator, during the course of the trial. "And he's come down to the Witness Room and led you out of the Witness Room and down the hall to talk to you about it, hasn't he?" Cole asked.

"Yes," Rountree replied.

"Did you understand that you were sequestered as a witness, that you were not supposed to talk to other people about your testimony except, perhaps, the attorneys in the case?" Cole asked.

"Well, I thought—thought he was an attorney," Rountree said.

"I see," Cole said. "Have other people been talking to him, too; has he been coming down there and getting other people while you've been in the Witness Room?"

"I think Ed Smith," Rountree said. Ed Smith was to be the defense's next witness.

Having established the possibility that the witness's testimony had been influenced, Cole asked Rountree, "And to tell the truth about it just without anybody refreshing your memory, you're not too sure which week we're even talking about back in 1972, are you?"

"No," Rountree admitted.

Ed Smith testified next for the defense. He was employed by Wilcox Advertising in 1972 but had been retired for five or six years at the time of the trial. He confirmed that he had seen Lorenzo Marshall in Albany on the night of Thursday, August 31st, and that they both slept in the same warehouse. He was riding in a separate vehicle, however, and said he returned to the Wilcox office in Valdosta about 4:30 Friday afternoon.

Lamar Cole cross-examined Smith about the details of his work in Albany. All went smoothly until he asked Smith, "Has somebody talked to you real recently about just this particular part for you to be sure you remember that Friday?" At this point Smith, who had a heart condition, complained of shortness of breath and asked for a break. As his testimony progressed, it became evident that the week he was talking about was not the week Hellen Hanks went missing. He admitted that the defense's investigator had called him out of the Witness Room earlier in the day, taken him to "an office" in the building, and questioned him. Smith volunteered to Cole, "He ain't asked me nothing about the truck." When asked about his interview by police earlier in the investigation, Smith said, "They treated me nice. Ain't no need in me telling like they didn't. I'd be telling a story."

It was late in the day by the time the two former Wilcox employees completed their testimony. Judge Lilly dismissed the jurors, instructing them to return the following morning. With the jury out of the courtroom, Lamar Cole moved to strike the testimony of Ed Smith, citing "the conduct of the defense in this matter." His basis for the motion was the violation of the court's instructions that the witnesses be sequestered and the defense sending a non-attorney (Doug Moss) to go over testimony with them during the course of the trial. Cook responded that Moss had merely sent for the witnesses and he himself had spoken with them "for about two minutes," denying that any rules had been breached. Lilly denied Cole's motion but warned the attorneys about such future conduct.

The defense's first day of trial testimony had ended. It was unclear that any progress had been made toward proving Keller Wilcox's innocence. Foxy Wilcox's testimony was at odds with that given by the police and other witnesses. Dr. Burton's expert testimony, while technically impressive, was at its heart a situation of expert versus expert with disparate interpretations of the meaning of the same evidence. Based on Lamar Cole's cross-examination, Buddy Yow's account of his visit to the Wilcox Advertising office appeared simply too convenient. The final two witnesses, Ellis Rountree and Ed Smith, were placed on the stand to provide Lorenzo Marshall with an alibi, and thus support his recanting his confession. Yet neither gave strong testimony, and possible (though denied) interference and/or coaching from the defense detracted from its value.

The next day would be critical. Keller Wilcox was scheduled to testify in his own defense.

Hellen Hanks was a thirty-four year-old happily married mother of three, employed as a secretary and bookkeeper for Wilcox Outdoor Advertising in Valdosta, Georgia. In this photo taken shortly before her disappearance in August 1972, Hellen's husband, James Hanks, is seated to her right. Fifteen year-old Lucy is in the left rear, with thirteen year-old David to her left, and ten year-old Penny in front. *Courtesy Hanks family.*

Hellen Hanks was employed by Wilcox Outdoor Advertising prior to her unexplained disappearance on August 31, 1972. This photo of the company offices at 701 East Hill Avenue in Valdosta was taken in July 1981 shortly after Foxy and Keller Wilcox were arrested and charged in connection with Hellen's murder and the concealment of her body. *Associated Press/Atlanta Journal-Constitution. Photographer: Bud Skinner.*

In the fall of 1979, more than seven years after their mother's mysterious disappearance, the children of Hellen Hanks erected this monument to her memory over an empty grave. It would be a year later that Hellen's remains were discovered, and nearly two years before their final interment near this monument. *Courtesy William Rawlings.*

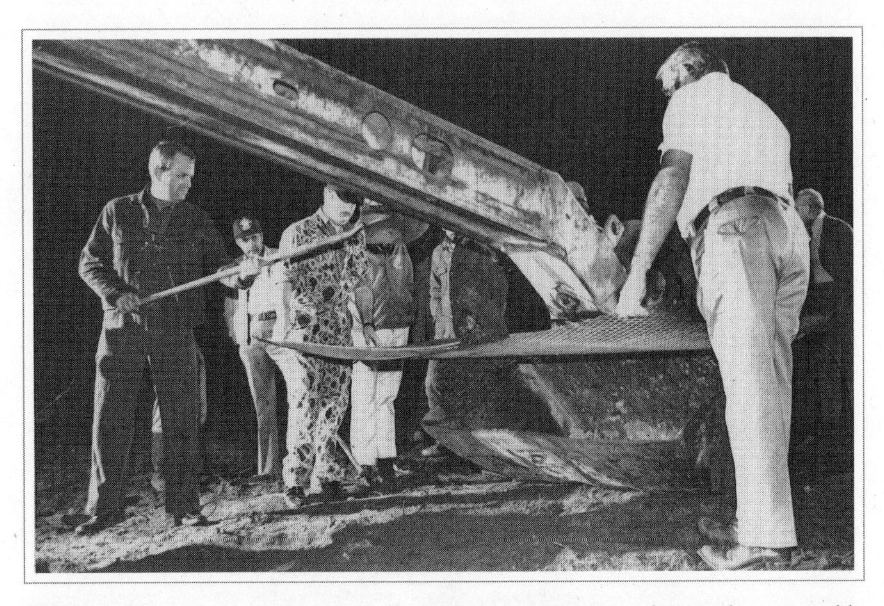

The November 24, 1980 discovery of a buried box containing human bones quickly led to the conclusion that these were the remains of Hellen Hanks, missing since August 1972. The fact that the box in which she was buried came from Wilcox Outdoor Advertising quickly cast suspicion on the owners and employees of the business. *Exhibit at trial of State vs. Wilcox (1982).*

Hellen Hanks's dismembered body was buried in a box from Wilcox Outdoor Advertising. The box, designed for heavy use on the back of a work truck, was covered in sheet metal. This helped preserve the victim's remains inside. *Exhibit at trial of State vs. Wilcox (1982).*

Valdosta, Georgia, Friday Afternoon, July 3, 1981

Valdostan Is Charged In Helen Hanks Death

By ARCHIE McKAY
Times City Editor

A Valdosta businessman was arrested early today and charged with murder in the 1972 death of Helen Griffin Hanks while his father and two others were charged with attempting to cover up a crime.

E.K. Wilcox Jr. of Castlewood Apartments, was charged with murder and a bond hearing was being held at mid-morning.

E.K. "Foxy" Wilcox Sr., 73, of 817 Mill Pond Road, was charged with hindering the apprehension of a criminal. He is free on $25,000 bond after an arraignment at Valdosta police headquarters this morning. Justice of the Peace George Hart held the arraignment.

Two former employees of the Wilcox family business, Wilcox Outdoor Advertising, where Mrs. Hanks was also employed, were also arrested and charged with hindering the arrest of a criminal.

They were identified as Lorenzo Marshall, 69, of 212 W. Branch St., and Ed Wrentz, 77, of Old Lake Park Road. Both remained in county jail this morning though bond was set at $25,000 each.

Superior Court Judge W.G. Elliott was to arraign the younger Wilcox at 10 a.m. and court observers speculated he would be granted bond.

The early morning arrests were made by Lowndes County Sheriff G. Robert Carter and Police Chief Loyce Arnold.

They and District Attorney Lamar Cole held an 8 a.m. press conference to announce the arrests following weeks of speculation and rumor about the case.

Mrs. Hanks, 35 at the time, disappeared from her job at the company Aug. 31, 1972 and at the time the case was treated as a missing person.

However, on Nov. 23, 1980, a man plowing a field southwest of Valdosta's airport turned up a box which turned out to be a make-shift coffin and contained the skeletal remains of Mrs. Hanks.

Following an all-night wrap-up, police and sheriff's investigators early today gave the green light to their bosses and the arrests were made.

Herman Griffin of Jesup, twin brother of the late Mrs. Hanks, who was formally buried only last week, was present during the night as investigators completed their work and the arrests were made.

Griffin was present at the press conference but did not speak.

However, asked earlier by a newsman if he was satisfied with the investigation Griffin said "yes."

The next legal step is a commital hearing, if defense lawyers request it.

Then, if enough evidence is presented to satisfy a magistrate, the cases would be sent to a grand jury which would decide if there is enough evidence to hold the four for trial.

No motive was given today for the slaying and the cause of death has not been pinpointed.

Arnold, Cole and Carter would give no details of the case.

However, the Times learned earlier the elder Wilcox and the two black former employees are accused of helping to bury the woman's body in the field, which in the early 1970s was a wooded area.

The body was found in a box later identified as the kind the billboard firm used to house materials in to protect them from the weather.

Investigators believe the woman was killed at the office on West Hill Avenue, put in the box and later, perhaps the next day, buried in the wooded area in a grave about four to five feet deep.

Capt. Billy Register of the police department and Lt. Billy Selph of the sheriff's department headed up the investigation of the slaying, assisted by other officers, including Sgt. Charlie Spray.

E.K. WILCOX JR.
Charged With Murder

E.K. 'FOXY' WILCOX
Free On Bond

"Valdostan is Charged in Helen Hanks Death." The arrest of two prominent citizens for a murder that occurred nearly nine years earlier sent shock waves through the local community. The Wilcoxes were quickly freed on bail while the two black former employees charged in the case remained in jail. *Valdosta Daily Times, July 3, 1981.*

E. K. "Foxy" Wilcox, Sr. was a wealthy and prominent member of the Valdosta community. At the time of Hellen Hanks's murder, he and his wife lived in this house near the county club in fashionable north Valdosta. *Courtesy William Rawlings.*

Charged with the murder and concealment of the death of their company secretary, the financial resources of Foxy and Keller Wilcox allowed them to hire the best defense counsel available. Wilby Coleman (left) and Bobby Lee Cook (right) are shown as they arrive for a pre-trial hearing at the Lowndes County Courthouse on July 24, 1981. *Associated Press/Atlanta Journal-Constitution. Photographer: Nancy Mangiafico.*

Famed defense attorney Bobby Lee Cook (left) discusses a point with Keller Wilcox's wife Sonia (right). *Associated Press/Atlanta Journal-Constitution.*

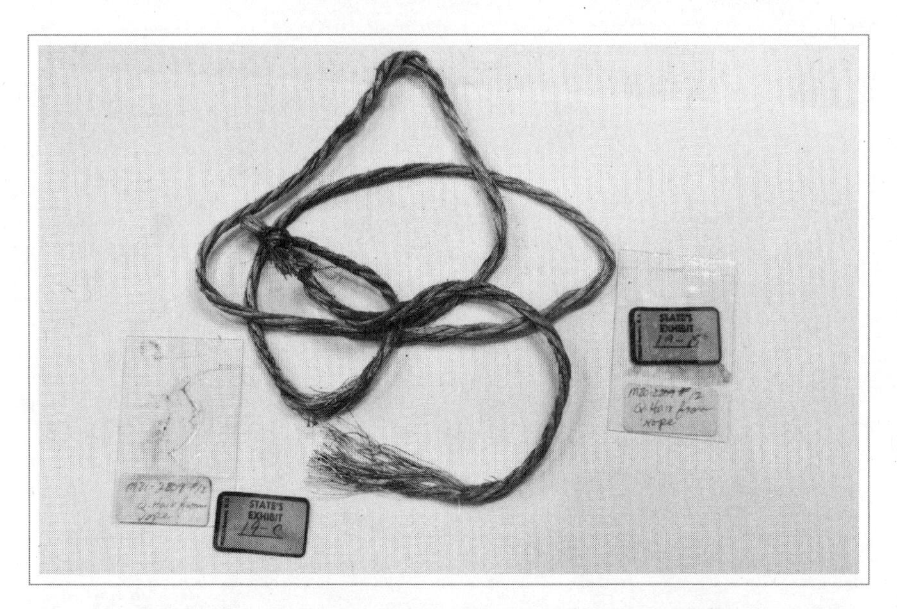

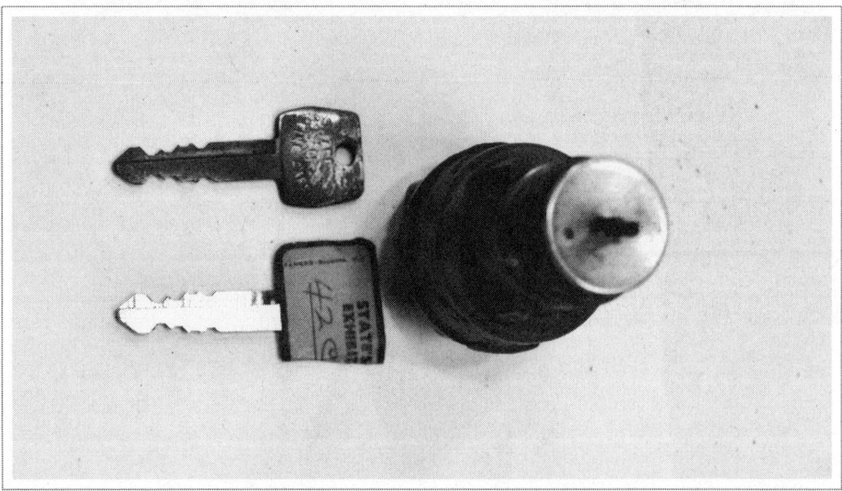

Two of the exhibits that appeared to assist the jury in reaching a guilty verdict in Keller Wilcox's murder trial are shown here. To the top is a length of rope the prosecution's experts theorized was used to strangle the victim. To the bottom is a key and an ignition assembly of the truck allegedly used to carry Hanks's body to the hidden burial site. There were only two keys to the truck, and Keller Wilcox was in possession of the other one. *Exhibit at trial of State vs. Wilcox (1982).*

The presence of the "stake-bodied truck" at Wilcox Outdoor Advertising on the day that Hellen Hanks went missing served to discredit the trial testimony of Lorenzo Marshall, an important prosecution witness who later tried to recant his earlier statement implicating Foxy and Keller Wilcox in the burial of Hellen Hanks's body. *Exhibit at trial of State vs. Wilcox (1982).*

Nearly four years after being convicted of the murder of Hellen Hanks, Keller Wilcox was ordered released from prison by Judge Wilbur Owens. Shown here with his wife Sonia, Keller is being interviewed by a reporter for the Atlanta Constitution in December 1985. Judge Owens's decision was overturned by the U.S. 11th Circuit Court of Appeals in the spring of 1987, returning Wilcox to prison. *Associated Press/ Atlanta Journal-Constitution. Photographer: Ken Klanicki.*

July 11, 2006

Dear Members of the Board:

I want to acknowledge and accept responsibility for the death of Helen Hanks on August 31, 1972. Ms. Hanks was my father's secretary. We got into an argument and I lost my temper. I did not mean to hurt her. There was never a sexual assault or anything like that. I was scared and told my dad what happened. I was working for my dad at that time.

I was not present when Ms. Hanks' body was buried in the field.

I am deeply regretful for the pain and suffering we have caused Ms. Hanks' family as a result of my actions on that afternoon. All the many years since that fateful afternoon I have tried to avoid bringing shame and embarrassment to my family by not admitting my responsibility. I am now 55 years old. It has been 34 years since Ms. Hanks' death. Now all my family members are deceased. Had I accepted the prosecutor's

On July 11, 2006, after more than a third of a century of denials of any involvement in Hellen Hanks's death, Keller Wilcox wrote a letter of confession to the Board of Pardons and Parole. His admission of culpability did not fit the known facts in the case, leading many to suggest that the "confession" was a cynical gesture designed to win his release from prison. He was freed on parole in May 2008. *Courtesy Hanks family.*

(continued on next page)

PAGE 2

offer and admitted my guilt I would have been released from confinement many, many years ago.

I have been a model prisoner during my 23 plus years of confinement. I have been a trustee / firefighter for the last 12 years. I want to be a productive citizen, possibly a firefighter, if I am released from confinement.

Thank you for your time considering this matter.

E. Keller Wilcox

Chapter 19

The Trial: Day 8 (Part I)—Keller Testifies

Wednesday, January 13th, was to be the last day of testimony in the trial. The cold weather of the preceding two days had given way to heavy rain with high temperatures in the low fifties, a miserable day to be outside. Lota Wilcox, the widow of Foxy's brother, was the defense's first witness. In very brief testimony, she gave the same account as Daisy Harrell, confirming that Foxy rode to the Ocean Pond party with her and other family members. Other than this information, her memory seemed to have failed her. She could not remember at what time they left for the event or when they returned home.

Diane Head testified next. She'd worked for Wilcox Advertising for about two years beginning in the spring of 1978. Miss Head stated that she and Keller "became friends" during her employment there, denying that he made "any sexual advances" toward her. She continued, "He was the utmost gentleman at all times. He even had, you know, several opportunities and he did not at all." When asked to expand on that, she explained that Keller had visited her apartment and she'd visited his home, but nothing happened. "We even went to Atlanta together on business. And he was at all times, just like I said, the utmost gentleman. I really admire him."[a]

---

[a] On later cross-examination by Lamar Cole, the following exchange took place: Cole: "Did you kind of—were you kind of disappointed that [Keller] never did make any advances?" Head: "No, sir, I was not." Cole: "The only advances that were ever made were made by you, you say?" Head: "No, sir, I wouldn't call them advances." Cole: "Nothing further," with which the cross-examination ended.

Other men weren't so polite, Head testified. "Mr. Neil Johannessen on several occasions made some rude comments, some advances that I thought were very inappropriate, that were offensive to me."

"Did he attempt to put his hands on you?" Wilby Coleman asked.

"Yes, sir, he did."

"And I believe you said Keller never did anything like that?"

"No, sir, not at all," Head replied.

The mention of Neil Johannessen, who had died nearly two years earlier of presumed autoerotic self-asphyxiation, was not random. As a witness for the defense, Diane Head would have discussed her testimony in detail with Bobby Lee Cook and Wilby Coleman prior to the trial. In his courtroom questioning, Coleman told Head to "be specific" when naming others who'd not been as gentlemanly as Keller Wilcox, no doubt expecting her to respond with Johannessen's name. There could be no rebuttal, as Johannessen was dead and died under unusual circumstances with sexual overtones. This may have been an attempt on the part of the defense to introduce the possibility of suspects other than their client.

The defense's next two witnesses, Tommy Strom and Carl Smith, had both worked at McGowan Funeral Home in the late 1960s and the early 1970s. Strom was the chief embalmer. At the time, funeral homes, rather than hospitals or municipalities, commonly provided local ambulance service. While a student, Keller Wilcox worked as an orderly at the Valdosta hospital, perhaps because of his initial interest in pursuing a career in medicine. It was there that he met Carl Smith, and through Smith, met Tommy Strom. There had been unsubstantiated rumors that Keller hung out around one of the local funeral homes and somehow this might have had some connection to the dismemberment of Hellen Hanks's body. There were other rumors, again unsubstantiated, that Hellen Hanks's murder might have involved necrophilia. Strom and Smith were put on the stand by the defense to dispel these vague allegations.

Strom testified that while Keller did visit the funeral home, it was mainly to hang out and visit with Carl Smith. To his knowledge, Keller never went in the embalming room where the work on bodies was performed. Smith stated that Keller did, however, ride on ambulance calls, "helping me pick up patients and carrying them to the hospital." Sometimes the ambulance picked up bodies at the morgue; Smith admitted Keller "may have went with us a couple of times."

In response, Lamar Cole asked, "And was there ever any, you know, in spite of the fact that the person was dead, dead men telling no tales, was there any horse play of any sort when Keller was around with any of those bodies?"

"Not that I know of," Smith replied.

Cecil Franklin, an agent with the Georgia Bureau of Investigation, was the next witness. There had been some uncertainty that he would be allowed to testify. Franklin was a polygrapher and during the GBI's 1972 investigation of Hellen Hank's disappearance had given a lie-detector test to Keller Wilcox.[b] Because of its well-established lack of reliability, information obtained via polygraph testing is not admitted as evidence in courts of law. After some consultation outside of the presence of the jurors, the judge agreed that Franklin could serve as a witness on the condition that he only state what questions he asked Keller and what answers he received. The mention of a polygraph or lie-detector test was forbidden. On examination and cross-examination by the attorneys for both sides, it was simply established that in 1972 Keller Wilcox denied that he had anything to do with Hellen's disappearance.

Loyce Arnold, who'd testified earlier for the state, was recalled to the stand by the defense. Questioned by both sides, his testimony

---

[b] The so-called "lie-detector test" is done using a polygraph instrument, something that measures pulse, respiration, blood pressure, and skin conductivity while a subject is being asked questions. Someone who administers a lie-detector test is referred to as a "polygrapher."

revealed nothing new. In asking him about travel times between Cordele and Valdosta, Lamar Cole was able to reinforce the fact that Foxy and Keller could easily have arrived back in Valdosta by 3:00 or 3:15 P.M. on the afternoon of August 31, 1972, rather than 4:00 as had been testified.

Carla Wilkerson, who'd worked as a secretary at Wilcox Advertising for about five and a half months in 1981, testified next. She'd worked directly for Keller and denied any "untoward activity" or sexual harassment on his part.

Leland Cothron, a member of the family that sold the 490-acre tract off Indian Ford Road to Fred Blanton, testified that the land was "heavily wooded" in 1972. At times the land and/or a tenant house on it had been leased, but there were no renters or occupants during the summer of 1972. The site where Hanks's body was buried could have been accessed by more than one route. Because Cothron had problems with trespassers hunting or dumping garbage, he'd put some posts up to block one access route, but found later they'd been knocked down. He admitted it was possible for several men to carry a box from Indian Ford Road to the burial site without major difficulty.

Herman Lyle, an ex-FBI agent, was called next. He accompanied Keller Wilcox and Bob Bolton to the burial site off Indian Ford Road on the evening of the discovery. Lyle, who described Keller as a friend whom he'd met in 1974 through Bob Bolton, had retired to Valdosta that same year after a twenty-seven-year career with the FBI.[c] All three men were members of the police auxiliary. The defense's apparent reason in calling Lyle as a witness was to imply that the recovery of evidence from the burial site was done haphazardly. His testimony did not confirm this. In an exchange on cross-examination by Lamar Cole in reference to Dr. James Howard's supervision of the scene, Lyle was

---

[c] Keller Wilcox indirectly implied in later testimony that he'd joined the police auxiliary in 1977 but said he'd had friends in the police department prior to that date.

asked, "And did [Dr. Howard] appear to be working slowly and carefully when he was working on that box, picking up bones and bagging them?"

"Ah, under the conditions I'd say he was doing an admirable job," Lyle replied.

"Meticulous?" Cole asked.

"Very meticulous."

The defense's final witness of the morning was Detective Captain Billy Register of the Valdosta Police Department. Together with Lieutenant Billy Selph of the LCSD, he had led the investigation after Hellen Hanks's remains were found. Bobby Lee Cook questioned him in detail regarding the interview of John Wesley Goodman, who had testified earlier for the prosecution. Goodman's interrogation took place four days after the discovery of the victim's body. Both Register and Selph were present. Goodman, with other Wilcox employees, was a potential suspect at the time. The main thrust of Cook's questioning appeared to be an attempt to discredit the way the investigation was conducted and to inject the issues of race and attempted intimidation of witnesses.

Citing passages from the typed transcript of the interview, Cook noted Register's threats of issuing a murder warrant for Goodman and that he would "hunt him to the four ends of the earth" if he did not return sober for a second interview. Cook demanded, "Can you name any white men that you told that to while you were interrogating [them], Mr. Register, yes or no?" Cook read passages in which Register told Goodman that he was going to "fry your ass," in which he "told him that you were going to put him in the electric chair," and in which he threatened to "hold [Goodman] indefinitely although you had no charges against him and no evidence against him."

On cross-examination Lamar Cole asked, "Well, were you just trying to pin this thing on Johnny Goodman or were you trying to find out what he knew?"

"No, sir, we were trying to gather information about the disappearance of Mrs. Hanks at that time, sir," Register replied.

Cole established that Goodman was a drinker and "drinking pretty well" at the time of his interview. Reading from the transcript, he brought up again Goodman's statement, "I saw the Wilcox boy slap Mrs. Hanks on the butt and she made a little swing like she was going to hit him. I heard him call her a name—like bitches and whores." Goodman said these events occurred in "the paper room," the same location that Lieutenant Billy Selph had earlier testified held the ropes and cutting shears.

Keller Wilcox was to be the defense's last witness. Bobby Lee Cook had promised in his opening statement to "put Keller Wilcox on the stand and subject him to a thorough and sifting cross-examination by Mr. Cole." It was a risky gambit. The press (and no doubt the jury) had already noted the discrepancy between Foxy Wilcox's testimony and that of the police, James Hanks, and others. As Foxy and his son were the only ones who knew the truth of their activities on the afternoon and evening of August 31, 1972, Keller would be forced to repeat the same basic story. Anything different would cast further doubt on his father's testimony, as well as his own. In the end, the jury would be asked to decide who was telling the truth and who was not.

Keller's initial testimony in response to Cook's questioning went smoothly. He recounted the events of the week of August 31st, including the business trip to Atlanta. He confirmed that Don Wright, the Wilcox employee from Albany who drove a car with an Alabama tag, had visited the company's Valdosta office in his absence on August 30th.

Sticking with the timeline Foxy had given, Keller reported that they left Cordele at "approximately two o'clock," reaching Valdosta "around four o'clock," and arriving at the local office between 4:15 and 4:30. He confirmed the presence of the three policemen and James Hanks and recalled Buddy Yow dropping by for a short while. He stated that his father, Foxy, was there the entire time and supported

Foxy's testimony that everyone left the office "around eight o'clock." Keller said he and his father departed in separate cars, and after going home and cleaning up, arrived at the Ocean Pond party at "eight-thirty to nine."

Keller denied the presence of "any trucks" (including the stake-bodied vehicle) in the office parking lot. He denied that he regularly drove the tan '71 Ford pickup, instead driving a company car the majority of the time.

When the Ocean Pond party broke up, Keller said he "went by the office to check and make sure that our office was locked up and secure." He didn't stay there long, he stated. In fact, the entire time between his leaving the party and his arrival at home was only "thirty to forty-five minutes." As his ex-wife testified earlier, she had fallen asleep, leaving no witnesses to confirm or deny his story.

In an apparent effort to show that Keller had access to family land on which he could have buried a body if he wanted to, Cook had him identify photos of two large and isolated tracts near Valdosta that might have served that purpose. Confirming the testimony of Tommy Strom and Carl Smith, Keller acknowledged that he'd worked as a hospital orderly during two summers while in high school but denied that he'd ever been in the embalming room at McGowan's Funeral Home.

Lamar Cole's cross-examination of the defendant began with a difficult question: he asked why, on the morning of his arrest, Keller had met the Lowndes County Sheriff and the Valdosta Police Chief at his door "with a gun in your hand?" This was the first time this episode had become public knowledge. This exchange was followed by a series of questions and denials: Keller denied driving the beige Ford pickup "after the summer of 1971," except occasionally on weekends. He denied ever "cussing" Hellen Hanks or that he had ever touched her at all. He knew of no reason why Ed Wrentz, Jerry Davis, Ed Smith, Johnny Goodman, and others whose testimony might have hurt his case would have anything against him.

Focusing on one of the key points in the state's case, Cole questioned Keller in detail about the exact timing of events on the afternoon and evening of the day Hellen Hanks disappeared. Traveling back on I-75, it was agreed that the distance between Atlanta and Cordele was about 160 miles and that the distance between Cordele and Valdosta an additional 90 miles. In 1972, Keller told the GBI that he and his father arrived in Cordele to visit with Willard King about 1:00 P.M. They had dropped someone off at the airport before 11:00 A.M. and had stopped once for gas, meaning they covered the 160 miles from Atlanta to Cordele in an estimated two and a half hours. King had testified earlier in the trial that he thought the two left Cordele for Valdosta at about 1:30 P.M.; Keller estimated it was half an hour later. Based on both Keller's and Foxy's testimony, they arrived back in Valdosta at around 4:00 P.M. If this time was correct, it would mean that Foxy and Keller covered the first leg of the journey (which included a stop for gasoline) at a rate of about 65 miles per hour. If *their* estimate of their time of arrival in Valdosta was correct, it would mean that they were traveling on the interstate at about 45 miles per hour or even *less* if Willard King's testimony was correct.

Complicating this timeline was Jean Johannessen's testimony. Lamar Cole asked, "Didn't you tell your wife at five o'clock on the day when it happened..., a little bit after five when she'd gotten home, didn't you tell her that, well, we got back between three and three-thirty, but there's something wrong here, Mrs. Hanks is missing and we've been looking for her and calling people...?"

"I don't know what I talked to her about," Keller replied.

"Well, you could very easily have been back between three and three-thirty, couldn't you?" Cole asked.

"If you left at two, giving yourself an hour-and-a-half, it would have been at least three- thirty then," Keller admitted.

Cole went on to point out that in an October 1972 interview with the GBI, Keller said they arrived back in Valdosta about three forty-five but now insisted to the district attorney that they arrived at the office "between four-fifteen and four-thirty." He did acknowledge that James Hanks arrived there about 5:25 or 5:30.

"Now if Jean King Wilcox Johannessen's testimony is correct that you got there between three and three-thirty," Cole asked, "then who was there between three-fifteen and five-twenty five? Who was there during that period of time?"

"I don't agree with her testimony that we got to the office between those times you just mentioned," Keller said.

"You heard her say that's what you told her on the phone?" Cole asked.

"I heard her say it," Keller stated.

"And you disagree with that?"

"Like I said a minute ago, my recollection is we got to the office between four-fifteen and four-thirty," Keller said, disputing the testimony of his ex-wife and in the process leaving up to two hours unaccounted for.

Keller again testified that the police arrived around 5:30 and stayed until approximately 8:00 P.M., noting again that Buddy Yow also "popped in" for a while. He was unable to explain why the police hadn't seen Yow. He said his father, who no one else had seen either, "was in and about the office the whole period of time."

Cole asked, "Was it still daylight when the police left?"

"At eight o'clock at night?" Keller asked.

"Yes, sir."

"It was dusk."

"Getting dusk," Cole said. "Isn't it true that your father drove off in that big Continental about the time you called for the police and before they arrived, isn't that true?"

"Repeat that, please," Keller asked.

"It's true, isn't it, that you and your father were there early in the afternoon before the police ever got there?"

"We were there together," Keller replied.

"And isn't it true that your father drove off in that big green car before the police got there?"

"No, sir," Keller said.

"And that he stayed gone until after the police were gone and then came back about six-thirty or a quarter to seven?" Cole asked.

"No, sir. He was there the whole time the police were there"

"And wasn't it true," Cole continued, "that between six-thirty and eight o'clock...there was some frantic activity between you and your father in getting something out of the back of that green car that had not been there while the police were there and getting it into the back of the warehouse and going and picking up some men and taking them out in the woods somewhere to do some digging?"

"No, sir," Keller answered.

"Well, what did you do between six-thirty and eight o'clock?"

"We were there with the police the whole time they were there in the office," Keller replied. Cole pointed out that his testimony was at odds with that of the GBI, his ex-wife, the police, and James Hanks, not only about the timing of events that evening, but also as to the presence at the Wilcox office of Foxy's car and the stake-bodied truck. Sticking to his story, Keller simply acknowledged his disagreement without offering an alternative explanation.

One of the questions that had remained unanswered throughout the trial was why Hellen Hanks's killers chose Indian Ford Road as the site to bury her body. The dirt road, which in 1972 was a ten- or twelve-minute drive from the Wilcox office and warehouse, had originally extended south from the outskirts of Valdosta before intersecting with Old Clyattville Road. When Interstate 75 was built in the 1960s, the north end of the road was cut off, after which Indian Ford Road dead-ended at the interstate right-of-way. As such, it provided convenient access to billboards erected along the interstate. Keller said he'd never heard of the road.[d]

One exchange between Cole and Wilcox about the Blanton property was of interest. Keller stated that while he was free on bail after his arrest, he'd gone there with Doug Moss, Bobby Lee Cook's investigator. In response to Cole's question about the location, Keller replied, "I remember seeing the FAA site[e] the night we rode down there, the night they found her in November of 1980, and it looked different with the land cleared and the land planted in 1981 than it did the night that we rode down there. So, I could only guess for the investigator where the site was."

Seemingly surprised, Cole asked, "Wait a minute now, you say it looks different now that's it cleared from what it used to?"

"The night we rode down there the land was muddy," Keller replied. "There were some stumps in the field. It was not planted. It was not cleared like it is right now, the night they found her and the night Mr. Lyle and all of us rode down there with the other law enforcement officers." Rightly or wrongly, some observers interpreted this as a slip on Keller's part, implying that the land in 1980 or 1981 looked different as compared to when Hellen's body was buried there in 1972.

In making a final point, Lamar Cole asked Keller, "Isn't it true that you got Hellen Hanks's key, the one to the gas pump and that pickup key and her office key right out of her pocketbook?" Keller denied this but did acknowledge that he'd received some keys from James Hanks, admitting, "She might have had the gas pump key."

---

[d] It should also be noted that for someone driving south toward the countryside from the Wilcox office, Indian Ford Road would be the first substantial dirt road one encountered after crossing the interstate. For someone wishing to dispose of a body quickly, it might be a logical place to turn off the highway to seek a secluded spot.

[e] The burial site of Hellen Hanks's body was near a Federal Aviation Administration (FAA) radio tower site on the Blanton property.

In almost every way, Keller Wilcox's account mirrored and supported that of his father. With formal testimony ended, it was evident that both had chosen to describe a different timeline for the events of the afternoon of August 31, 1972. If the Wilcoxes were to be believed, there were few unaccounted-for moments between the time they returned to Valdosta from Atlanta and the time they arrived at the wedding party at Ocean Pond. The collective testimony of the state's witnesses, however, gave strong support to the contention that their activities between about 3:30 and 5:30 P.M., and again between 6:30 and sometime around 8:00 P.M., were unknown. It was during those times, the state contended, that Hellen Hanks was murdered and her body hidden until it could be buried.

Chapter 20

The Trial—Day 8 (Part II): Closing Arguments

The trial was nearing the end. During six long days the jury had listened to more than fifty witnesses. The state had introduced some fifty-five exhibits as evidence, the defense more than a hundred. There had been accusations and denials. There had been conflicting testimony, all given by individuals sworn to tell the truth. It would now be the task of the panel of twelve men and women to sort out, to the best of their ability, what appeared to be true and what did not.

Prior to turning the case over to the jury, Judge Lilly charged them with their duty:

> *Ladies and Gentlemen of the jury, at this time the case has been closed by both sides. That is, all of the evidence is in, the witnesses have been excused and the attorneys for both sides, the State and the Defendant, will be addressing you in concluding arguments.*
>
> *An attorney in presenting his argument to the jury has a right to reflect upon the evidence, to comment upon the evidence, to give his interpretations of...the meaning of the evidence. I want you to understand that the conclusions or interpretations which the attorneys draw and these interpretations are not binding upon you.*
>
> *While the attorney has a right to draw his conclusions from the evidence, you are to carefully consider the evidence and reach your own conclusions as to its meaning, and you are not bound by the interpretations which the attorneys place upon the evidence.*
>
> *This is a useful and very worthwhile part of the trial of any case to allow counsel for...each side to address the jury and call to the jury's attention his interpretation of the meaning of the evidence and the conclusions to which the evidence, he feels, points.*

Dwight May would speak first for the state, followed by Wilby Coleman for the defense, and then Bobby Lee Cook. The district attorney, Lamar Cole, would speak last. Each had his own style; each had its own agenda, but the goal of all presentations was convincing the jury of the defendant's guilt or innocence.

Dwight May described for the jury the state's theory of events on the afternoon of August 31, 1972. He pointed out that witnesses had testified that Keller had made sexual advances to Hellen Hanks, advances she rejected. As a result, "There was friction between the two of them." Again, based on trial testimony, he noted that Foxy and Keller could easily have gotten back to Valdosta from their Atlanta business trip by 3:00 or 3:30 P.M. Here his narrative deviated from the defendants' statements, who alleged they'd gotten back into town around 4:00 or 4:30. It had been established that the police and Hellen's husband did not arrive at the Wilcox office until nearly 5:30 P.M. In two very long sentences, May went on to describe what the prosecutors believed happened during the two hours or so prior to that:

> *But I submit to you that you can logically deduct from the evidence in this case that they arrived back in Valdosta, Georgia—give them thirty minutes—at 3:30, that they were driving Mr. Wilcox's large automobile, that at that time Keller drove his father to his house, his father got out and Keller got his automobile and drove down to the business and I believe that you can logically deduct from the evidence that Keller got down there and found Mrs. Hanks working on her books.*
>
> *And I also believe that you can logically conclude or deduct from the evidence that they had a greeting and may have discussed the trip and at this time Keller Wilcox under some pretense got Mrs. Hanks back to the paper room and at some time or another he did what he had done before, he made an advance on Mrs. [Hanks] and she rejected it and she slapped him and he cursed her and he reached down in a bucket and picked up a rope and put it around her neck and he strangled the life out of Mrs. Hanks and then he did whatever those folks do when they are making a sexual assault on another human being, but in this case he had before him a lifeless body and I submit to you the evidence shows that he took a pocket knife or he took some shears that you've seen photographs of, that you've heard testimony about in this case and he proceeded, on State's Exhibit One, the green dress, and he took those*

> *shears and he cut her sleeves all the way up to her neck on both sides and he took that dress and peeled it down her body and he cut her bra from her body and he skinned Mrs. Hanks like you might skin a snake and when he got her fully naked, when she was nude, Keller Wilcox did whatever it is those folks do in a sexual assault and of course we don't know whether or not he raped her because all of her flesh had rotted from her body when it was discovered in the late fall of 1980.*

Realizing what he had done, May theorized that Keller then called his father, who immediately drove to the Wilcox office. Comprehending the magnitude of the problem, they put Hellen's body in the trunk of Foxy's Lincoln. Foxy then left, while Keller notified James Hanks and the police. May emphasized that while both of the Wilcoxes testified that everyone remained at the office until around 8:00 P.M., neither of the two police officers who were there nor James Hanks recalled seeing either Foxy or his green Continental. The officers and Hanks also testified that they left between 6:00 and 6:30 P.M. May pointed out James Hanks's testimony that he found Keller searching Hellen's pocketbook and that Keller was given some keys from it. These keys, May suggested, were the one for the gas pump and the spare key for the '71 Ford pickup that were later found in the grave.

May continued his theoretical narrative as to what transpired next:

> *The law enforcement officers are gone, Mr. Hanks is gone, and there is nobody at the business but scared, frightened Keller Wilcox and we know what his Daddy's been doing, his Daddy's been getting some help from two employees that he could absolutely trust, that they did exactly what he told them to do without question or talk. And he came back in his automobile and he got these two black employees and they loaded up on a truck and drove out in the country and...commenced to dig a hole. They wouldn't dig that hole for Keller Wilcox because Keller Wilcox, the evidence has shown, was not nice and polite to the employees and he was a young man and they didn't have any respect for him anyway because he—the evidence shows he had not matured and they didn't feel he deserved respect, but they were doing this for Foxy Wilcox, their lord and master, the man that signed their check and they picked it up every Friday. Now...the time was approximately 7:00, 7:15 or*

> *7:30, they commenced to dig a hole. And the testimony has been in this case that after the hole got approximately three feet deep or maybe a little deeper, it started to rain.... They got rained out. They could not finish their work and they loaded up on a truck and they went back to town and parked the truck and let those two black folks out and those two black men, ladies and gentlemen, were not told why they were digging the hole.*

After returning to town, May continued, Foxy and Keller drove home, cleaned up a bit, and went to the party at Ocean Pond. "They couldn't have been dirty," May said, "they couldn't have been that dirty anyway because Ed Wrentz and the other black man did all of the work and they just stood around and told them how deep to dig and how big to dig the hole and they watched them. They weren't that dirty when they left because they didn't do anything, but at any rate, we know they were late for the party."

After leaving Ocean Pond, May hypothesized that Keller did not go directly to the office, but instead went to his father's house after Foxy had been dropped off there by his relatives. They picked up Ed Wrentz and Lorenzo Marshall and went back to the Wilcox office. "The work they had to do there, ladies and gentlemen, was to fix Mrs. Hanks's body so it could be hidden in the box because rigor mortis had set in." Her legs were cut off, put in the box, and the box nailed shut there in the warehouse. "Somebody reached down and picked up her bundle of clothes and when they did that the padlock and the gas switch [key] got tangled up in them, because undoubtedly they filled up that truck before they left there that night and they had to unlock the gas switch to fill it up because they weren't going out anywhere and run out of gas and the keys were picked up and they were entangled in the dress. Keys to a '71 Ford pickup truck, the padlock itself and the keys...."

"When they finished their dirty work," May continued, "they got back in the truck and drove back to...their office building, and they got off the truck and the two black men walked home, Keller took his Daddy home and Keller went home. It could've been 3:00 in the morning for all we know, 4:00 in the morning, because his wife testified she didn't know what time Keller got home. He didn't wake her up."

Later, May addressed the effect on the Hellen Hanks's family:

> *Can you imagine the agony of the Hanks family? Can you imagine what those folks went through? Those young children? When all of a sudden their mother disappears from the face of the earth? Can you imagine the agony and frustration James Hanks went through? Can you imagine the agony and frustration the Griffin family went through all of these years while her body was concealed from her family and lying in an unmarked grave in Lowndes County, Georgia. And as Providence would have it, one day a man clearing some land...."*

In closing, May addressed the issue of race, referring to it as a "red herring" thrown out by the defense.[a] "Race has no place in this case at all. We've got a white victim and a white defendant and race, Mr. Cook hopes, will anger some of you because of what the law enforcement officers did. And he wants you to get so mad...that you'll forget about the evidence in this case. And I submit to you that race is not an issue, and has no place in this case whatsoever, none."

Wilby Coleman spoke next on behalf of the defense. He began his presentation on a note of hyperbole, referring to the case as "one of the, perhaps, the strangest and most convoluted prosecutions maybe in the history of the court system." He referred to Dwight May's closing arguments as "postulation and speculation" akin to "Fantasy Island." But in contrast to May's chronological presentation of the state's theory of the case, Coleman's was more rambling, attacking the

---

[a] A "red herring" is something—a clue, evidence, allegation, or the like—that is used as a diversionary tactic in a search for the truth. The term is attributed to William Cobbett, an early nineteenth-century English journalist who used the example of a "red herring" (a smoked fish with a pungent odor) being used to lay a false scent trail when training hunting dogs.

investigation in general and peppered with personal attacks on the investigators and the opposing attorneys.

Coleman began by accusing news media coverage of fanning public interest in the case after the discovery of Hellen Hanks's body. This, in turn, led to pressure on the police to name a suspect or make an arrest. "They had zeroed in on Keller Wilcox at some point because of the fact that allegedly Keller Wilcox made a pass at Mrs. Hanks." Following this thread, investigators focused on Wilcox employees. "Now, so what they did was commenced to bring hard pressure on those who they considered the weakest of the Wilcox employees who were...the oldest and the ones with the least education and they were black.... They wanted to be able to pressure them by force, intimidation and to implicating their oldest [employers] and friends, the Wilcoxes, in this crime. That was the sole purpose for Ed Wrentz and Lorenzo Marshall to have been subjected to the absolute abhorrent conditions that they were."

Calling the police liars and their reports falsified, Coleman sought to discredit their testimony, which was damaging to his client's case. He cited how Keller appeared "perfectly normal" at the Ocean Pond party, further evidence that he could not have committed such a heinous crime. "The state has pulled in witnesses from all over the place, all over the country coming to testify in this trial, but they have not produced one witness who said that Keller Wilcox was in a state of panic, shock, overexcitement or anything else that night. Not one. Not a witness."

Continuing, Coleman questioned why material identifying Wilcox Advertising was buried with the body. The state contended that the missing cash boxes and bank bag were taken and buried perhaps to make it appear that Mrs. Hanks had been kidnapped following a robbery. "That's like putting a tag on a corpse and saying 'I just killed Jane Doe, sincerely yours, John Doe.' It makes no sense," Coleman contended. And as to the burial site, he pointed out that it would have been safer for Keller to bury a body somewhere on the several hundred acres of family land to which he had access.

Seeking to cast suspicion on other suspects, Coleman brought up the name Glen Gregory, a man who had rented the Blanton property at one time (but was not renting it when Hellen Hanks was buried there). He again spoke of the mystery man driving the car with the Alabama tag that allegedly had been seen at the Wilcox office on the day Hanks vanished. Even though the state seemed to have reasonably established that the man was Don Wright, a Wilcox employee, and that he'd been there on the 30th, not the 31st, Coleman clearly hoped this would sow more seeds of doubt. He criticized investigators for not doing more to follow up on this potential lead.

In criticizing Lamar Cole, Coleman said,

> *The District Attorney, in his closing argument, is going to try to convince you of some very strange things. I want to point them out to you beforehand. I think you'll hear them from his lips, or a lot of them, perhaps in modified form. He's going to tell you that when you don't have any defense, what you do is try the police. And we're not trying the police here, ladies and gentlemen; we're exposing the lies, the immorality, the illegality and unconstitutionality of the actions of the state in this case. It is the most incredible instance of it that I have ever seen.*

With that premise, Coleman went on to attack several of the state's witnesses, reserving his harshest words for the police interrogation of Ed Wrentz and Lorenzo Marshall, whose original testimony—if believed—was among the strongest pillars of the state's case. "I think it's rather pathetic that the police would turn these two old, honest men against their longtime friends. I think it's absolutely pathetic. And they did it in a very systematic way which was known in the early thirties in Nazi Germany as the storm trooper method."[b]

---

[b] Coleman compared Wrentz's and Marshall's interrogation to *Kristallnacht*, which the court reporter recorded as "crystal nic." *Kristallnacht*

In closing, Coleman said, "I'm going to simply say to you that this is one of the greatest miscarriages of justice that I have ever seen attempted to be perpetrated by the state. Keller Wilcox is absolutely—absolutely—innocent of these charges and there has been absolutely no proof that he committed any crime whatsoever. Not one single fact to indicate the commission of a crime."

Bobby Lee Cook spoke next. Exactly one month earlier, a writer for *Atlanta Weekly* magazine had described him as "Shakespeare in legal clothing and a master of improvisation in the courtroom."[94] In contrast to his sometimes-bombastic cross-examinations, Cook chose this time to adopt a more nuanced approach, one that seemed to reflect sadness that the trial was even taking place. He began on an academic note, quoting several cases addressing the level of proof needed to sustain a conviction based on circumstantial evidence. Setting the tone for the rest of his remarks, he quoted a 1943 opinion from Supreme Court Justice Felix Frankfurter: "A democratic society in which respect for the dignity of all men is central naturally guards against the misuse of the law enforcement process. Zeal in tracking down crime is not in itself an assurance of soberness of judgment. Disinterestedness in law enforcement does not alone prevent disregard of cherished liberties."[95]

Moving on, Cook expressed his appreciation to the people of Valdosta, stating, "I have never been treated with any more courtesy or with any more sincerity than I have in this community." He complimented the jurors: "You are obviously a jury which is highly intelligent." He praised the "American form of government," contrasting it with "governments which lie abroad and especially behind the Iron Curtain."

Cook spoke of the "presumption of innocence" as it applied to Keller Wilcox, pointing out that the burden of proof fell entirely on

(German for "Crystal Night") refers to the nationwide attack on Jewish properties, homes, and synagogues that took place in Germany on November 9–10, 1938.

the state. The defendant, he noted, was not required to present witnesses or take "the stand, even in his own defense." Referring to Chief Loyce Arnold's 1972 missing person summary Cook noted, "There is not any mention in this report, not the slightest indicia[c] or a word which would indicate that there had been any harassment, sexual or otherwise, at the job site by Keller Wilcox or anyone else."

Investigators deliberately ignored the issue of the car with the Alabama tag, Cook alleged. "The couple across the street, according to the uncontradicted evidence in this case—and the state can turn and twist and wiggle all they want to—but it comes back to the fact that these two people were the last people in Valdosta that saw Mrs. Hanks alive on August 31, 1972. And there hasn't been a single diligent effort made to locate those two individuals."

At this point, in an apparent attempt to inject some levity, Cook told a joke about his uncle Roy and a bird dog that he sold for five dollars to man during the Depression Era.

Continuing, Cook said,

> *I feel sorry for a lot of people in this case. I certainly feel sorry for the Hanks family. I feel sorry for the Wilcox family who have suffered the slings and arrows of outrageous misfortune.*[d] *I feel sorry for Ed Wrentz, and Lorenzo Marshall and John Goodman.*
>
> *And I don't mind telling you that I would be dishonest if I didn't tell you that it makes my blood boil and it makes me upset when I hear anyone say that I'm going to act as the judge and I'm going to act as the jury and if you don't do what I say do I'm going to punish you. And I've tried cases throughout this country for thirty-three years, and I have never seen anything in my thirty-three years that reeked, reeked*[e]

---

[c] "Indicia" (Latin: signs): When used in a legal sense, refers to signs or indications that something is probable, but not certain.

[d] Here Cook is misquoting Shakespeare's *Hamlet,* Act 3, Scene 1. Hamlet: *To be, or not to be, that is the question: Whether 'tis nobler in the mind to suffer the slings and arrows of outrageous fortune, or to take arms against a sea of troubles.*

[e] Here the court reporter transcribed "wreaked." The spelling is corrected.

> *with such sadness, and such desperation and such pervasive overreaching as I have seen in this case.*
>
> *Many of our...older people fought a war that lasted a long time to preserve what we're talking about and what this system is all about and if we could look now the beaches of Iwo Jima, Okinawa and Omaha would still run red with American blood to protect [these] liberties that are essential to continuing [the] safeguards of a democratic institution.*

These words served as a lead-in for an attack on the investigators' interrogation of Ed Wrentz. The bedrock of the state's entire case was Wrentz's testimony, Cook implied. It was so tainted by police misconduct that it could not be considered, making the state's case worthless.

In closing, Cook vaguely implied that a person or persons unknown had murdered Hellen Hanks and buried her body: "There is no evidence in this case from which you can conclude beyond a reasonable doubt and to a moral and reasonable certainty that Keller Wilcox or anyone else identified killed the deceased in this case." Waxing eloquent to the jury, he closed his oration by saying,

> *The saddest epitaph which can be written by free people is that free people didn't stretch out their hands to save the liberties and constitutional safeguards in this country while there was yet time to do so. Two hundred years ago a bunch of young folks, people a lot younger than some of us on the jury and myself, were writing our Constitution up in Philadelphia and they had been laboring for a long time and young Benjamin Franklin was walking down the steps of the Continental Congress and a...young lady came up and said, "Well, Mr. Franklin, what sort of government have you given us?".... Ben Franklin said, "My dear madam, I gave you a republic that we can keep." I thank all of you for your patience, and I ask you in this case, that based upon the evidence, not based upon sentimentality, not based upon charity, not based upon pride, that you render a verdict in this case which speaks the truth of this transaction, and that's the verdict of not guilty. You are not responsible for the consequences of your verdict, you're only responsible for the truth of your verdict. And there's an old saying that if you're true to yourself, you cannot be false to any man."*

Cook thanked the jury and sat down.

Bobby Lee Cook had been polished and articulate in condemning the state's case while defending his client's innocence. It was now up to Lamar Cole to present the prosecution's final arguments. He began by responding to Cook's closing:

> *How much have you heard about the rights of Hellen Hanks? Certainly we're here to enforce the Constitution, but Mr. Cook is not the sole arbiter of the Constitution. He's not the only one that can tell you about that, and even though he may be impressive, ladies and gentlemen, how much did he talk to you about the rights of Hellen Hanks?*
>
> *He says, "Oh, I'm not here to impress you. Far be it from me," he says. Can you tell that the man has studied off at the defense schools to flatter you by telling you how many times he did that you're intelligent and well-chosen and so forth?*[f] *Can you tell he's had elocution and speech training because he raises his voice like that and then gets it down to a whisper?*
>
> *I'm going to forget all that stuff in a minute, ladies and gentlemen, and just talk to you, and I may get excited and talk fast. I may slow down and have to scratch my head and think of what I was going to tell you. But let's talk about the facts: How much time did Mr. Cook spend telling you about his Uncle Roy, about the Founding Fathers, about the Star-Spangled Banner and quoting Shakespeare about the slings and arrows of outrageous fortune? Did he tell you about the tangled web we weave when we first practice to deceive?*[g] *Somebody is trying to deceive you about this case and sure they got it all messed up.*

---

[f] With the term "defense schools," Cole is referring to training that trial attorneys often take to improve their courtroom skills, including speaking to jurors.

[g] In repeating the phrase "the slings and arrows of outrageous fortune," Cole is correcting Bobby Lee Cook's earlier misquote from Shakespeare's *Hamlet*, Act 3, Scene 1. (See footnote XX.) The "tangled web" quote is from Sir Walter Scott's 1808 romantic poem "Marmion."

> *One of the last things that was said to you by the defense was, well, if anybody's going to do a murder, why would they do it in such a dumb fashion and leave clues all over the place? Well, somebody did it, didn't they? And whoever it was didn't intend for it to be found out. Didn't you hear that testimony, another six inches and none of this stuff would have been found? He didn't intend to leave clues all over the place. Why do it in a dumb fashion? Crime is dumb. It's not only mean and rotten and wrong, it's stupid to start with and it's not planned often.*

Cole described Hellen Hanks's murder as a crime of "passion," a crime of opportunity that was not planned in advance. He spoke at length about the evidence and the defense's efforts to introduce "straw men," suggesting there were others—as yet unknown—who were responsible.[h] However, as Cole pointed out, "whichever man or men that participated in this thing, they used not only Mr. Wilcox's rope, Mr. Wilcox's building, Mr. Wilcox's box, Mr. Wilcox's padlock and key, but they even left his truck key out there and still had one truck key left."

The district attorney voiced his concerns about the conduct of the police in interrogating potential suspects. In doing so, though, he asked the jury, "Does that excuse this man for taking the life of this poor woman?" He spoke of the uncertainties of some of the testimony on both sides, but rejected the defense's assertions that many of those who testified for the state were "liars."

In acknowledging that the case against Keller Wilcox was a circumstantial one, Cole pointed out that the crime of murder was often one in which there were no witnesses. And there were unknown details: "Now we don't know for sure if [Hellen Hanks] left there in the trunk[i] and came back later. We don't know for sure if she was buried late that night or the next night.... Ed Wrentz can't tell you and I can't tell you and we don't have to know. She was killed there by a person who had

---

[h] The term "straw men" as used here is equivalent to the term "red herring."
[i] Cole is referring to the trunk of Foxy Wilcox's green Lincoln Continental.

the means, the motive and the opportunity, and I submit to you a person who was already sexually attracted to her and whom she had rebuffed. She was killed there on that day and hid somehow and buried later."

In closing, Cole said, "Ladies and gentlemen, it's a circumstantial evidence case with strong circumstances that point to no other conclusion than the guilt of Keller Wilcox on both counts, and we ask, please, that you find him guilty."

Judge Lilly thanked the jurors, dismissing them until 9:00 A.M. the next morning. It would be that day that Keller Wilcox's fate was decided.

Chapter 21

The Trial—Day 9: A Verdict

The morning papers of Thursday, January 14th, were subdued in their commentary on the previous day's testimony. There were snippets and brief quotes, most frequently Keller's complete denial of guilt. The jurors would have the case before the day was out. That was the real news story; everyone was waiting on their decision. Spectators continued to pack the courtroom as the rain slacked off and the weather turned cooler once again.

The evidentiary portion of the trial was over. The next scheduled items on the agenda were Judge Lilly's charge to the jury followed by the panel's deliberation. The judge's charge had been carefully written in advance and approved by both the prosecution and the defense. The charge would outline for the jury the exact nature of the offenses for which Keller Wilcox was indicted and instruct the panel in their options and obligations in reaching a verdict. Prior to the jury's return to the courtroom, however, Bobby Lee Cook offered two hand-written, last-minute changes, both aimed at blocking the jury's consideration of the testimony of Lorenzo Marshall and Ed Wrentz. Lamar Cole responded, pointing out that the defense had adequate opportunity to offer up such changes earlier in the proceedings. Judge Lilly agreed, rejecting Cook's motions. It was clear that the defense saw these witnesses' testimony as a threat to their client.

With the jury back in the courtroom, Lilly began by explaining the basics of the two crimes with which Keller Wilcox was charged, carefully noting that he had pleaded not guilty to both. "The guilt of the defendant must be proved beyond a reasonable doubt," the judge instructed. "It must not rest upon conjecture or mere suspicion. Where all the facts and circumstances of the case and all reasonable deduction therefrom present two theories, one of guilt and the other consistent with innocence, the justice and the humanity of the law compel the acceptance of the theory which is consistent with innocence." Lilly emphasized that the burden of proof fell upon the state; the defense had no obligation to prove anything.

The judge reviewed the essential elements necessary to convict the accused of murder: First, it must be established that the presumed victim is actually dead. Second, it must be shown that the victim's death was caused by violence or "criminal agency." Finally, it must be shown that the accused caused the death. He emphasized that it was up to the jury to determine the veracity of witnesses, to reconcile differences in testimony, and to weigh the value of evidence presented. Lilly spoke to the special considerations necessary when determining guilt or innocence in a case based on circumstantial evidence.

In conclusion, Lilly advised the jurors, "You are the sole judges now of not only the facts, but of the law, as the law should be applied in this case. The facts are that you're the sole and exclusive judges of the facts and the law now. You're the sole and exclusive judges of the guilt or innocence of the accused." Court was adjourned as the jurors were dismissed to the jury room to begin their deliberations.

Approximately two hours passed before the jury sent word that they had reached a verdict. It was a remarkably short period of time, given the gravity of the crimes and the complexity of the trial. It suggested that whatever the outcome—guilt or innocence—the members of the jury had reached a firm conclusion by the end of trial testimony.[a] Judge Lilly warned the spectators, "There shall be no demonstration of any kind from any one."

The jury returned to the courtroom. "Members of the jury," Lilly asked, "have you reached a verdict?"

---

[a] An anonymous member of the jury panel, speaking later to a reporter researching the case, "explained that in truth the decision took only about 'as long as it took to drink a Coke.'" (James Dodson, "The Second Life of Keller Wilcox," *Southern Magazine* [November 1986].)

"We have," the foreman replied and was instructed to hand the verdict to the judge, who read it silently.

"All right." Lilly said. "I'm going to ask the Clerk to publish the verdict. The defendant will rise and face the jury."

The clerk read, "As to count one, we, the jury, find the defendant guilty. As to count two, we, the jury, find the defendant guilty. This January 14, 1982, James A. Rogers, Foreperson." The room was quiet in stunned silence.

Judge Lilly inquired if either side wished to examine the verdict. Instead, Bobby Lee Cook requested that the jury be polled. Each of the twelve jurors individually answered, "Yes, sir" to the questions "Was this your verdict?" and "Was it a free and voluntarily entered verdict?"

The jury was dismissed as Judge Lilly prepared to sentence Keller Wilcox. He inquired of Cook if he wished to make any statement on his client's behalf. The defense attorney said only that he intended "to immediately, of course, file a motion for a new trial" but had nothing more to say.

Lilly asked Keller Wilcox if he wanted to make a statement. The reply was a simple, "No, sir."

"Very well," the judge said. "With respect to count one, it's the sentence of the Court that Mr. E. K. Wilcox, Jr...., the jury having found you guilty of the offense of murder, and the sentence of the Court is that you be committed to the Department of Offender Rehabilitation and that you serve in the penitentiary a sentence of life imprisonment, the remainder of your life." For count two, concealing a death, the judge imposed a sentence of an additional twelve months, "to be served consecutively to the sentence" of life in prison. After a brief final discussion of Keller's right to appeal, Judge Lilly instructed the sheriff to "take the defendant into custody." A shocked Keller Wilcox, dressed in a tan suit, white shirt, and striped tie, was led away in handcuffs, his head bowed. His aunt, Hyta Mederer, who had worn a fur coat to the trial, was heard to comment, "You know, that just kills me. They don't have to handle him that rough."[96]

"And when the formal proceedings of the court were completed, emotions were no longer contained," the *Valdosta Daily Times* reported. "Friends and relatives of the Wilcox family found it difficult to overcome their shock, and fruitlessly tried to console each other. On the other side of the room, tears flowed freely as members of the Hanks and Griffin families embraced each other. Wilcox's father, E. K. "'Foxy' Wilcox Sr. also accused in the incident, sat in a stupor, his face flushed in disbelief as others around him expressed their dismay that 'an innocent man could be found guilty....'"[97]

Wilby Coleman admitted he was shocked by the verdict. "I can't conceive of how it was arrived at." As to his client, Coleman said, "He's stunned. You can imagine how he's taking it.... I know I would be scared if this had happened to me." He said an appeal bond would be sought, confidently predicting that "the process would probably take at least two weeks."[98]

Bobby Lee Cook suggested that "the very poor and those that are at least assumed to be very wealthy have one thing in common. Although it is for different reasons, they both have difficulty getting a fair trial."[99]

On the other side of the courtroom, the family of Hellen Hanks was jubilant. "The Griffin brothers—tall, brawny and red-faced—embraced at the news Wilcox had been convicted in the death of their sister," the *Atlanta Constitution* reported. "Lucy Hanks, the pretty daughter of Hellen Hanks, hugged the detectives who had investigated the case. 'I told her I'd never back off this case,' said Deputy Billy Selph. 'I don't think she'll ever forget that.'"[100] "Herman Griffin, [Hellen Hanks's] twin brother, said he spoke for the family as he tearfully expressed, 'Thank God for that chisel plow—thank God!'"[101]

What happened? The *Times*'s reporter, who'd followed the trial closely, commented, "The case seemed to be favorable for the defense throughout most of the prosecution's case.... But with the first witness for the defense, the tide appeared to change. The senior Wilcox's testimony contradicted the timetable given by several other witnesses. As his testimony continued, he became somewhat belligerent and was admonished by the judge for swearing. The testimony by Dr. Joseph Burton, chief medical examiner in DeKalb and Cobb Counties could not overcome the impact made by Dr. Larry Howard of the [state] crime lab."[102]

Other evidence and other witnesses seemed to have played an important role in the jury's decision as well: Buddy Yow's testimony suggesting that Hellen Hanks was missing at midday on August 31st was considered suspect. Keller Wilcox's statement that the burial site somehow "looked different" when he visited the site after the body was found may have been important to the jury. The keys and padlock found in the gravesite and their connection to the keys from the victim's pocketbook "provided [the jury] with a strong link to the crime." "The defense's ploy to use what they described as racial discrimination on the part of law officers involved in the case was turned and used against them as the state intimated the elder Wilcox abused the trust in him of two elderly black employees by having them assist in covering up the murder."[103]

"Many believe the jurors' minds were probably set by the time [Dwight] May gave the state's detailed rendition of Mrs. Hanks's death in his closing arguments. It is difficult to say what items, blatant or subtle, may have influenced the verdict of the eight women and four men who were given the task of determining another's fate."[104]

A reporter for the *Florida Times-Union* commented, "It was the perception of power and wealth, as much as the facts in the case, that sparked such intense interest. 'People said the Wilcox money would buy him off,' Herman Griffin, Mrs. Hanks's twin brother, said after the trial was over."[105] The *Valdosta Daily Times* reporter agreed, but pointed out that the facts, presented by a team of civil servants, had yielded a verdict of guilty: "To be sure, money was in evidence as you looked at the defense table. Cook's six-figured fee is as renowned as his courtroom prowess. Three other lawyers were seated with him as was a special investigator, while the state's table had two public employees, namely District Attorney Lamar Cole and Lt. Billy Selph of the Lowndes County Sheriff's Department, and Dwight May, a special prosecutor hired by Mrs. Hanks's family."[106]

A week after the end of the trial, the *Daily Times* published a long letter to the editor from "Doc" Griffin, another of Hellen Hanks's brothers. Speaking on behalf of the families, he thanked the members of law enforcement who investigated the case and the attorneys who presented it in court. Responding to an earlier editorial[107] in the paper that highlighted Bobby Lee Cook's fame and fees, Griffin wrote,

> *The District Attorney and Mr. May do not have the national reputation and do not receive the fees which your editorial attributes to Mr. Cook. However, they presented the evidence in a competent, methodical, legal manner. We were proud of the fact that they stood their ground and were not awed by Mr. Cook.... It strikes us that the real lesson to be learned from this trial is that no matter how good the defense attorney may be, or how high the fees he may earn, in the final analysis it is how the members of the jury view the evidence in the case when they go to the jury room. We are satisfied that by their verdict of guilty, justice was served.*[108]

Chapter 22

Aftermath—A Bond Hearing and a Lawsuit

With the trial over and Keller Wilcox's sentence of life in prison handed down, there appeared to be few in Valdosta who had not formed an opinion of the case. Deferring to the jury's verdict, and perhaps influenced by media reports, most thought a murder mystery had been solved, justice had been served, and a just punishment prescribed. There were others, though, including many of Keller's friends, family, and acquaintances, who simply could not believe that he was capable of such a crime, that his conviction and sentence were miscarriages of justice. This would become evident at the appeal bond hearing held before Judge Lilly twelve days after the end of the trial.

Prior to this, however, on January 20th Keller's attorneys filed notice of an appeal of his conviction. Wilby Coleman, ever aware of the role the media had played in covering the case, told a reporter for the *Daily Times* that the appeal would be based "on the general grounds that the state did not carry the burden of proof beyond a reasonable doubt." If an appeals court overturned Keller's conviction, "the state could only try him again if it had newly discovered evidence." Coleman said he'd "already discovered a dozen" grounds for appeal, including failure of the court to grant a trial delay in order to examine the audio tapes of Jean Johannessen for evidence of tampering. While those appeals worked their way through the court system, Coleman had requested a hearing to allow his client to remain free on bail.[109]

The appeal bond hearing was held on January 26th at the courtroom of the Lowndes County jail, where Keller had been held since the end of the trial.[a] Keller, this time dressed in a blue prison jumpsuit, was represented by Wilby Coleman. Lamar Cole represented the state. Unlike the trial, in which the burden of proof was on the state, in this proceeding it would be the defendant who would be required to convince the judge that his client's release was appropriate under the circumstances. Coleman had scheduled six witnesses, the state none.

Hyta Mederer, Keller's aunt and the person who'd posted his bond after his arrest in July 1981, took the stand first. Her testimony consisted simply of acknowledging that she was willing to post bond for her nephew, should the judge decide to grant it.

Keller spoke next. Under Coleman's questioning, he denied that he was a flight risk or that he would attempt "to approach or talk to any of the witnesses in this case" should he be released. To establish his ties to the community, Keller said that he was vice president, secretary, and general manager of Wilcox Outdoor Advertising, that he was (or until recently had been) a member of the boards of directors of the Valdosta Touchdown Club, the Valdosta Boys Club, the Outdoor Advertising Association of Georgia, and the Valdosta Chamber of Commerce. He was a member of an advisory committee to the president of Valdosta State College and served on a committee of the Outdoor Advertising Association of America.

On cross-examination by Lamar Cole, Keller admitted that his father had two valid airline tickets to Canada for himself and his son at the time of their arrest but asserted these were for a fishing trip planned well in advance. Although he denied any prior direct conversations with any of the witnesses who testified at his trial, Keller admitted that he had been present when Bobby Lee Cook's investigator, Doug Moss, had spoken with them. He admitted speaking to his ex-wife, Jean

[a] The proper legal term for appeal bond is supersedeas bond. If granted in this case, it would allow Keller to remain free on bond under certain conditions until his conviction was overturned or until he had exhausted his appeals through the court system.

Johannessen, prior to trial but said he couldn't recall talking about any issues that came up in court.

John B. Lastinger, the executive vice president of the Valdosta/Lowndes County Chamber of Commerce, spoke next on Keller's behalf. He admitted knowing Keller "since he was born" and that he coached him in Little League Baseball. Lastinger said he was certain that Keller would not try to flee or intimidate witnesses.

To Lamar Cole, Lastinger admitted Keller was a "personal friend" and that he was biased toward him as a result of that. Cole asked, "Then you don't personally believe he's guilty?"

"Well, no I don't," Lastinger replied.

"Regardless of what the jury says?"

"Well, you know," Lastinger said, "I don't because he looked me in the eye and told me he didn't do it."

Worth Green, Keller's dentist since age five, testified next, describing him as "a friend and a patient." Green admitted that he'd discussed the case with Keller and that he "absolutely" believed what he'd been told. Green did not think Keller would violate any conditions of his release.

As had the witnesses who preceded him, Dr. G. J. Austin, Keller's pediatrician, his godfather, and cohost of the Ocean Pond wedding party, testified that the now-convicted murderer was not a flight risk and unlikely to intimidate witnesses. Despite the jury verdict, Austin stated to Cole that "I certainly do not have any knowledge that [Keller] committed a crime." His chief justifications for this statement were, "I didn't see it happen" and "I haven't seen the evidence." He also admitted that he did not attend the trial.

Neil P. "Buck" Thomas, a retired school principal who'd known Keller in junior high school, described him as "a friend." He anticipated no problems if Keller were to be released on bond. Lamar Cole asked, "And really, the reason you have these conclusions about him is just because he's your friend, is that right?"

"If you can't look after your friend, well, there's not much to you really," Thomas replied.

The last witness for the defense was Virginia Wisenbaker, a guidance counselor at Valdosta High School. She had known Keller since prior to his first marriage and had introduced him to Sonia Lasseter, who would become his second wife. Wisenbaker testified that based on her education and experience, she was a good judge of people: "If I had any idea or any doubt of Keller's character or that he was the kind of person that could commit a crime I certainly would not have introduced him to Sonia." She added, "Keller Wilcox would not hurt anyone." On cross-examination, Lamar Cole asked, "Oh, what you say is, then, that you don't believe that he's committed a crime, not that you've never known him to commit a crime?"

"I've never known him to commit one," Wisenbaker replied, "therefore, I do not believe that he has committed one."

Lamar Cole delivered a relatively brief closing argument. He noted that Judge Lilly had presided over the court trial and was familiar with the case. He pointed out that Keller Wilcox had been convicted of murder, a crime of violence, and of concealing a death, "an interference with the administration of justice." In doing this, Keller sought the assistance of other persons, referring to his father as well as Ed Wrentz and Lorenzo Marshall.

In regard to the witnesses who testified on Keller's behalf at the hearing, Cole described them as good and well-meaning people but implied that their friendship had clouded their judgment of the possible consequences granting bond. "Judge, I don't charge them with any untruth whatsoever, but with an excess of love. As someone has said in making a mistake in judging someone's character, think of them as a person who loved not wisely, but too well."[b] In summary, he said,

---

[b] Here Cole, the former English major, is paraphrasing Shakespeare from *Othello*, Act 5, Scene 2. In this scene, Othello has just murdered Desdemona: Othello: "When you shall these unlucky deeds relate, speak of me as I am;

> *I just ask Your Honor to consider that even though they are quite worthy people, their beliefs are not well founded. The nature of this crime shows that this man did in fact do violence, that he concealed it over a period of time by devious methods that interfered with the administration of justice continually, and that he is capable of doing it again, Your Honor. Now we submit for these reasons, Your Honor, that there would be a danger to society if he should be released, that there's been no competent evidence to the contrary.*

Wilby Coleman based his closing arguments on two basic premises. First, Keller Wilcox's release on bond would represent neither a risk of flight nor a danger to current or potential witnesses against him if the case were to be retried. Second, Coleman presented a long list of what the defense team considered trial errors, including the failure to grant a continuance of the trial for the forensic examination of the audiotapes, the uncertainty at trial and defense's objections to the "means and method" of Hellen Hanks's death, the overruling of the defense's voir dire objections to certain members of the jury panel, the admission at trial of what Coleman termed "hearsay" regarding Wilcox's "sexual harassment" of the victim, et cetera. In essence, the grounds for requesting an appeal bond were the same as those that would constitute the basis of an appeal for a new trial.

Judge Lilly denied the request for bond, stating,

> *The defendant has been sentenced to serve the remainder of his life in prison for murder and twelve months for the offense of concealing death. Now, that's a dismal outlook and future for a man of the age of the appellant here, and the court cannot find that the appellant would not flee and does not find that he would not flee. The court finds that he very well might flee.*
>
> *Count Two of the indictment for which the defendant was convicted, that of concealing death to prevent discovery, of whether or not the*

---

nothing extenuate, nor set down aught in malice. Then must you speak of one that loved not wisely, but too well."

> *deceased was unlawfully killed is by the very nature of that crime a crime which obstructs justice...and the court finds that upon consideration of that crime there is a likelihood that the defendant might commit an additional crime of obstructing justice.*
>
> *The court finds that some witnesses have been influenced or intimidated before giving their testimony on behalf of the defendant and the likelihood is that there would be additional exposure to the intimidation of witnesses. From the evidence of the trial the court finds that there is a likelihood that the defendant would, if released on bond pending appeal, would commit other crimes and the court needs only to consider, as the jury did, the brutality of the crime for which the defendant was convicted in Count One to make the finding, and the court does make such finding.*

Keller Wilcox would remain incarcerated while his case was under appeal.

If for any reason one imagined things could not get worse for the Wilcoxes, they did. On January 26th, the same day on which the appeal bond was denied, James Hanks and his children, Lucy, David, and Penny Hanks, filed suit against Keller and Foxy Wilcox for the wrongful death of Hellen Hanks. Dwight May, who had assisted Lamar Cole at trial, and his law partner, Richard Goolsby, attorneys from Moultrie, brought an action against both father and son requesting $2,000,000 for the "mutilation and fraudulent concealment of the body from the family" plus an additional $202,000 from Keller alone for the wrongful death of their wife and mother. Asked for comments, local attorneys in Valdosta contended such suits were not uncommon but unusual in that the appeals of the case had not yet been settled. One lawyer commented, "A criminal case is fought with kid gloves, but in a civil case you can inject such things as character.... It (the suit) could be a wide-open, no-holds-barred hearing." Asked for a comment, Foxy said, "I don't know anything about it. I will have to see it first." There was no comment from Keller. He remained in jail as the slow appeals process began.[110]

Chapter 23

The Labyrinth of Appeals

Having lost his first attempt at freedom through a bail bond, Keller Wilcox remained in the Lowndes County jail while his attorneys prepared to file a series of appeals. At the most basic level, they sought two things: First, that Keller be released from incarceration while the validity of his conviction was under appeal in the court system. Second, that the jury verdict be thrown out as invalid, based on what his attorneys alleged were multiple errors in the trial proceedings, including problems with the jury, the conduct of investigators, the witnesses, the evidence, and the verdict under the law, to name a few.

The appeals process is one of the murkier areas of judicial practice. While the outcome—the hoped-for reversal of some verdict, ruling, or penalty—might seem clear, arriving at that point oftentimes requires a complex and expensive journey through the labyrinth of the court system. The terms used to describe the word "labyrinth"—complicated, tortuous, a complex branching pathway with multiple choices of direction—are appropriate.[a] Not only are there multiple hierarchal systems of courts, e.g., local, state, federal, but the rules and rights vary under each court system. In regard to the Wilcox case, one jurist noted, "State prisoners do not have an absolute United States Constitutional right pending appeal of their state court conviction."[111] On a federal level, however, the Eighth and Fourteenth amendments become pertinent, respectively banning "excessive bail" and stating that no state may

---

[a] In classical Greek mythology, the Labyrinth was a complex structure on the island of Crete built by Daedalus for King Minos to imprison the Minotaur, a half-human, half-beast creature that subsisted on human sacrifice.

"deprive any person of life, liberty, or property, without due process of law."

On June 15, 1982, the headline on the *Valdosta Daily Times*'s front page read, "Fed Court Will Be Asked to Free Wilcox on Bond." Blaming the court reporter for the delay in completing transcripts of both the trial and the bond hearing, Wilby Coleman declared that Keller Wilcox's "right to bond has been curtailed." Hoping to speed up the process, he had requested a hearing before US District Judge Wilbur Owens in Macon, Georgia. On the same day, Lowndes County Sheriff Robert Carter was served with papers demanding that he and Wilcox, accompanied by District Attorney Lamar Cole, be at Owens's chambers for a hearing at 11:00 A.M. on Friday, June 18th.

A *Daily Times* photo on the day of the hearing shows Keller leaving the Lowndes County jail dressed in a dark coat and wearing a striped tie. He was shackled in handcuffs and appeared to have grown a moustache while incarcerated. Pleading before Judge Owens on behalf of their client, Coleman and Bobby Lee Cook contended Wilcox's "Constitutional right to a speedy appeal" had been violated. Worth Green, Keller's boyhood dentist, and Lamar Wansley, the second host of the August 1972 party at Ocean Pond, testified on Keller's behalf. Owens refused to grant the Wilcox defense team's request for bail, primarily based on the fact that he had not exhausted his state court system appeals. He did, however, give the Georgia Supreme Court until August 10th to hold an appeal bond hearing. Coleman claimed victory, interpreting the judge's response "to mean he felt there is no ground for refusal of the bond."[112]

On the same day that Keller Wilcox and his defense team were in Macon, it was announced that the lawsuit filed against the Wilcoxes by the Hanks family had been dropped. In his initial response shortly after the action was filed, Wilby Coleman ridiculed the suit, stating that it was "incorrectly worded and must be redrawn, cutting out some information or be thrown out of court." He indicated that he was likely to request a change of venue and objected to "mention of mutilation of the body and any reference to the conviction of Keller Wilcox or the fact that he is now in county jail."[113]

In dropping their action against the Wilcoxes, Dwight May told the *Valdosta Daily Times*:

> *"There were two reasons the family decided not to pursue the suit. One was emotional and the other financial. He said they felt having gone through the murder trial was traumatic enough. May said they had begun taking depositions for the civil suit and the family was unable to handle many of the questions that were asked about their family, becoming very emotional at times.*
>
> *The Hanks [family] felt they were not financially able to handle the case, according to May. "We got indications from [the Wilcox lawyers] that it would take a lot of money because they were going to interview everyone in the case. They just did not have the money to fight the Wilcoxes," he said.*[114]

The reputed deep pockets of the Wilcoxes had carried the day.

Wilby Coleman, however, had another view of the situation. Speaking to a reporter years later, he recalled that Hanks dropped the suit "like a hot potato" after James and Lucy Hanks were deposed. "We took depositions for most of the day. During the depositions, my best recollection is both [James] Hanks and Lucy Hanks contradicted testimony earlier given in the murder trial and contradicted each other to such an extent that...after the transcript was done and they could see what position they were in, they figured they better get the hell out of there, and they just up and dismissed it."[115]

On July 8th, lawyers for both sides were notified that the transcript of the bond hearing had been completed. The case would be heard before the Georgia Supreme Court in a matter of weeks. Wilby Coleman was almost nonchalant in speaking with a reporter about the chances of success. "I don't believe there is anything that warrants a denial of bond," he said. As to the appeal of the verdict, Coleman was confident about this as well, though he admitted the process would be "long and involved." Quite sure of the eventual outcome, he declared his certainty that his client would be freed. In the meantime, he said, "I just hate to see the man in jail."[116]

Looking beyond the upcoming bond hearing, Coleman continued to fight his case in the press. In another interview with the *Daily Times*, he declared "the jury in the case was biased, and there were more than a dozen other errors in the trial serious enough to warrant a new trial." He pointed to two possible outcomes: "If the conviction is reversed by the court on the basis of one of the errors the defense says occurred in the trial, there would be a new trial, according to Coleman. If it is reversed on general grounds, he said there would be no new trial unless there was new evidence the district attorney could present, and Wilcox would be freed." Coleman did not mention the possibility of the failure of his client's appeals.[117]

On July 30th, the Georgia Supreme Court denied Keller Wilcox's appeal for release on bond pending the appeal of his conviction. Wilby Coleman was unavailable for comment.[118] Within days, the matter was back in federal judge Wilbur Owens's court. After meeting with both sides and hearing arguments, he refused to intervene, waiting instead on the outcome of appeals to the Georgia Supreme Court.

The true goal of Keller Wilcox's appeals was to have his conviction overturned in such a way that he could not be retried for Hellen Hanks's murder, barring the very unlikely possibility of the state discovering new evidence. Like all American citizens, he was protected by the so-called "double jeopardy" clause of the Fifth Amendment of the United States Constitution. This amendment, part of the Bill of Rights, was written to give criminal defendants certain protections against overreaching prosecution. In enumerating these rights, the clause states, "Nor shall any person be subject for the same offence to be twice put in jeopardy of life or limb," which means, in essence, the state cannot keep retrying a defendant until it gets the verdict it wants. If Wilcox's case were reversed because of insufficient evidence, for example, a new trial would be unlikely.

On Tuesday, October 12, 1982, the Georgia Supreme Court heard Keller Wilcox's appeal of his conviction. "Conflicting and illegal testimony and prejudiced jurors should result in either a dismissal of charges or a new trial," Wilby Coleman contended. The defense's appeal was based on three major grounds. First, Jean Johannessen's testimony should not have been admitted, as it violated the rule of marital confidentiality. Second, Judge Roy Lilly allowed jurors who "already had opinions in the case" to be seated, refusing to allow the attorneys during voir dire to ask "which way they were leaning." Third, the evidence in the case was insufficient; "Wilcox was never proven guilty of either the crime of murder or concealing death."[119]

The defense's arguments focused heavily on the testimony of Ed Wrentz. Bobby Lee Cook declared "police conduct in investigating the murder case was as 'shocking, as barbaric as any I have ever witnessed.'" Wrentz's confession was obtained only after he was "interrogated hour after hour without counsel...and threatened with lynching, with being lynched if he didn't tell [the police] what they wanted to be told.... Without the testimony of Wrentz, 'the evidence in this case does not support a verdict of guilty,' Cook contended."

In response, Lamar Cole "denied that police had acted improperly in questioning Wrentz, and contended that there was enough circumstantial evidence and testimony from other witnesses to justify the conviction."[120] "Cole said conflicts in Wrentz's testimony occurred because of the witness's physical condition. "He was uncertain simply because he was an old man and he simply did not want to remember those things because they were upsetting. We think although he appeared uncertain in certain areas...he was still a believable witness." Additionally, other evidence found at the burial site pointed to Wilcox's guilt. Apparently scoffing at Cole's argument, Wilby Coleman said, "What he is saying is that somebody killed [Hellen Hanks] so somebody has to suffer."[121]

The court gave no indication as to when they would rule on the appeal. Back in Valdosta, Keller Wilcox began his tenth month of incarceration.

Chapter 24

Setbacks and a Friendly Judge

On March 18, 1983, some fourteen months after Keller Wilcox was convicted of the murder of Hellen Hanks, the Supreme Court of Georgia affirmed the trial court's judgment. In a long and detailed unanimous decision, the court rejected the defendant's assertions that his conviction was invalid based on several errors at trial.

Keller Wilcox's lawyers contended "that the evidence against him was entirely circumstantial and did not exclude every other reasonable hypothesis except that of his guilt, and that the evidence was insufficient to support a conviction." The court found that in "reviewing the evidence in a light most favorable to the jury's verdict, we conclude that a rational trier of fact could reasonably have found the appellant guilty of the murder of Hellen Hanks and the subsequent concealment of that murder beyond a reasonable doubt..., and could reasonably have found that the evidence excluded, beyond a reasonable doubt, every other reasonable hypothesis except that of the appellant's guilt."

The court acknowledged the police's use of "some questionable interrogation techniques, such as trickery, intimidation, and isolation" while admitting "it is difficult to judge the extent of their use from the limited excerpts available." In alleging that Lorenzo Marshall's statement and testimony should have been excluded, the court concluded that the defense should have raised these issues at the time of trial, hence they were considered moot on appeal. Related to this, the defense also alleged that the trial court should have granted "a directed verdict of not guilty on the ground that the investigation of the appellant involved police misconduct so fundamentally unfair and shocking that it violated due process." The court pointed out that such interrogation might have been a violation of the rights of the non-defendant witnesses, which was remedied at trial on cross-examination in open court of these same witnesses. It was then up to the jury to decide on their credibility.

The court dismissed the claim of juror bias, finding the trial judge had handled this issue properly. Regarding the claim that Jean Johannessen's testimony should be excluded, the court found that although Keller and Jean Johannessen were married at the time, her testimony was admissible as it did not involve confidential communications between a husband and wife.

Wilby Coleman immediately filed a request asking the state Supreme Court to reconsider its unanimous decision. "We think there are substantial violations to due process guaranteed in the Constitution. Each of the six grounds on which we filed our appeal is founded on the right to due process. Yes, we definitely will go to federal court."[122]

Coleman's request for a rehearing of the case was denied on March 30, 1983. "Our contention is that the (Georgia) Supreme Court did not apply the law correctly or misinterpreted it...including the general grounds that the state did not prove his guilt," Coleman said. "They have only one witness that said [Wilcox] did anything, and he turned around and said he did not do anything."[123]

His appeals through the state court system denied, Keller Wilcox was transferred to the Georgia Diagnostic and Classification Prison near Jackson, Georgia, on May 10, 1983. His stay there was relatively brief. By early fall Keller had been transferred to the Jack T. Rutledge Correctional Institution in Columbus, Georgia.[a]

Keller Wilcox's imprisonment and the Georgia Supreme Court's rejection of his appeal seemed to have brought a sense of finality to the case. Enough, at least, to justify an account of the crime in the November 1983 issue of *True Detective* magazine. Under the teaser headline on its front cover of "Georgia's Eight-Year Murder Mystery Solved,"

---

[a] Columbus is located in Muscogee County, Georgia.

the article was titled "Blood Rage of the Too-Passionate Groper!" Despite the lurid title, it was a relatively tame and mostly factual account, probably sourced in large part from the Supreme Court's written decision of a few months earlier. In seven pages of three-column, small-font text, illustrated by photos of the burial box, Lamar Cole, Billy Register, and Billy Selph, the article presented the details of the crime as described in court, with a definite slant toward the prosecution's narrative. Jean Johannessen, Ed Wrentz, and Lorenzo Marshall were given pseudonyms; other major figures in the story were not.

The same month, Wilby Coleman filed suit in the Muscogee County (Georgia) Superior Court alleging the discovery of new evidence in support of the claim that Keller's "murder conviction should be thrown out." It had been discovered that one of the jurors in the trial had, at one time, been a police commissioner. The juror did not reveal this at the time of jury selection. Since part of the defense's planned strategy would be "antagonistic towards some of the police officers involved in the case," Coleman said they would have "struck him from the jury" if they'd known, alleging the juror's potential bias in favor of the state. In an additional bit of convolutional reasoning, Coleman said Ed Wrentz should not have been called as a witness by the state. The district attorney, he alleged, knew Wrentz "would say Wilcox was involved and later deny it. They knew he was going to perjure himself," Coleman said. "You can't say yes he did and no he didn't and not be guilty of perjury."[124]

On November 17, 1983, Muscogee County Superior Court Judge Kenneth Followill denied Wilcox's attorneys' appeal. On April 25, 1984, the Georgia Supreme Court declined to review this decision, finally exhausting all state court remedies and setting the stage for appeal through the federal court system. In September 1984, an appeal was filed in federal court in Valdosta, thus moving the case to a higher level.

Months passed. Keller remained imprisoned in Columbus. In early May 1985, in response to the request filed the previous year by his attorneys, Judge Owens requested that the Georgia Supreme Court deliver to him all of the trial records, exhibits, tape recordings, and interviews from Keller Wilcox's 1982 trial. Owens said he was "studying the entire record" and intended to have a hearing on the matter in the near future. He was particularly interested in "the sufficiency of the evidence in support of the conviction for murder" and the details of the interrogation of the witnesses. In his letter to the court—with copies to Coleman and Cook—Owens said he would "further entertain a motion from the petitioner that he be released on bail pending a final resolution of his...case."[125]

A preliminary hearing with the attorneys from both sides was held in US District Court before Judge Owens on May 16th. Coleman and Cook represented Keller Wilcox, with Assistant Attorney General William Hill representing the state. In addition to repeating their contention that police interrogation violated their client's constitutional rights, the defense attorneys claimed that they had "never seen" some of the audiotapes turned over to the court in response to Judge Owens's demand. "This is in complete violation of Judge Lilly's order that all tapes be turned over.... We've never been shown these tapes. They turned over nine tapes to us. They had twenty-one they didn't turn over."

In response, Lamar Cole, who was not present at the hearing, said "there were some tapes that the police had which were not placed in evidence by either side, but were exhibited to the defense. Maybe Mr. Coleman has forgotten that he was shown these tapes. They were shown a bunch. They chose not to use them all.... There has been a suggestion throughout the trial and the appeals that the police were engaged in various forms of misconduct, including the hiding of evidence," Cole said. "If that were true, why would the police now bring forth these tapes? If the police had concealed any such tapes thus far, why would they bring them forth at this time?"[126]

After the state produced documentation that Wilcox's attorneys did, in fact, have access to the tapes, the defense dropped any action based on the assertion that the state had withheld evidence in the form of audiotapes. They "probably would have had no effect on [our] defense in [the] case," Coleman said.[127]

At the May 16th preliminary hearing, "Owens expressed concern about the adequacy of the state's evidence against Wilcox. 'I don't have much trouble buying the fact that a murder occurred. But what shred of evidence do you have to link this human being to it?'" Owens asked Assistant Attorney General Hill. Bobby Lee Cook stated that he was "appalled" by the interrogation tactics used by police, telling Judge Owens, "Not only did they admit it on the stand under cross-examination, but they said they were proud of it and they would do it again." Based on both sides' presentations, Owens scheduled a full judicial review of the Wilcox case for early July.[128]

The second hearing was held on July 9th in Macon. Keller Wilcox, dressed in a white prison uniform, was present, as were Lamar Cole, officers Billy Register, Charlie Spray, and Billy Selph, as well as Ed Wrentz, now eighty-one years of age. Since the trial in Valdosta four and a half years earlier, Lorenzo Marshall had died of natural causes.

Bobby Lee Cook questioned the police officers "intensively" about their interrogation of suspects prior to Keller Wilcox's arrest, earning him "at least five rebukes from Judge Owens." Ed Wrentz testified that "he didn't know anything about the murder," stating he was in Florida at the time. He also stated that "he could not remember telling the police that he helped bury the body" but "disputed the defense contention that police used threats and scare tactics to get him to testify against Wilcox." During the 1982 trial in Valdosta, Wrentz's testimony yielded important yet contradictory testimony about his involvement in the disposal of Hellen Hanks's body. Terming him an "accomplice" (though he had been granted immunity), Judge Owens asked why his initial denials had not been presented with his later admissions.[129]

Observers of the hearing sensed that Judge Owens had serious doubts about the validity of Keller Wilcox's conviction. No date was given for when he might deliver his ruling.

Chapter 25

Freedom and a Firestorm

The headline on the front page of the December 22, 1985, edition of the *Atlanta Journal-Constitution* read, "Keller Wilcox's Murder Conviction Overturned."

> *A federal judge on Saturday threw out the 1982 murder conviction and life sentence of prominent Valdosta businessman Keller Wilcox and ruled he could not be tried for the crime again. U.S. District Court Judge Wilbur Owens, Jr. ruled there was insufficient evidence to convict Wilcox of the 1972 murder of Hellen Hanks, thirty-five year-old* [sic] *secretary and bookkeeper at Wilcox Outdoor Advertising, a company owned by Wilcox and his father. He also held that Wilcox's right to due process was violated when police officers used threats and intimidation to coerce statements from witnesses in the case.*
>
> *Because of insufficient evidence, "The state is thus barred from retrying the petitioner," Owens ruled. Wilcox could only be retried if the ruling is overturned, the judge said.*
>
> *"He feels vindicated but he regrets that four years of his life have been shot," said one of Wilcox's attorneys, Wilby Coleman of Valdosta, after informing his client by telephone of Owens's decision.*[130]

Owens also ruled that, pending any appeal by the state, Wilcox could be released on bond. If the state had an objection to his release, it was given seven days in which to present it. Potentially, Keller could be freed before the end of the year.

Foxy Wilcox seemed ecstatic. "Having him home is the greatest Christmas present ever," he said. "It's wonderful that the truth has finally come out."[131]

Georgia Attorney General Mike Bowers said his office would have to review the ruling before deciding whether or not to appeal the case.

Lamar Cole told a reporter that he would ask Bowers to appeal the ruling. "I think Mr. Wilcox had a complete and fair trial," Cole continued. He said it would be very difficult to retry the case "because one of the key witnesses (Marshall) is dead [and] another one, a quite elderly man (Wrentz), is four years older and his memory is getting foggy." As to opening a reinvestigation of the murder, Cole said, "The case was very thoroughly and adequately investigated the first time."[132]

Owens's decision was a shock to all but Keller Wilcox's most diehard supporters. It was unusually long—seventy-two pages—of which more than half were reproductions of transcripts of the police questioning of Johnny Goodman, Ed Wrentz, and Lorenzo Marshall. Owens's main reasons for overturning the conviction, however, referred to "insufficient evidence" for conviction. Specifically, he postulated that there were other possible suspects, suggesting Foxy Wilcox could have been upset when Hellen Hanks complained about having to keep "two sets of books." Perhaps she threatened to expose him, Owens theorized, so to prevent this, he killed her. In addition to this, Owens stated, "The only testimony linking [Keller Wilcox] with Ms. Hanks's death (the testimony of Wrentz) cannot be taken as true by a rational jury."

The insufficient evidence issue alone was all that was necessary to throw out the conviction. But, Owens continued, "even if the court were mistaken concerning the sufficiency of the evidence claim, petitioner is nevertheless due a new trial due to police misconduct." This, he stated, "'shocks the conscience' and thus violated the petitioner's rights under the Due Process Clause."[a]

Reactions to the news that Keller's conviction had been overturned were at polar extremes, depending on the individual's

---

[a] In referring to "the court," Owens is speaking of himself, using what some grammaticians refer to as the "fourth tense." The Due Process Clause refers to individual protections afforded under the Fifth and Fourteenth amendments of the Constitution.

relationship to the case. "We've won, hands down," said a jubilant Wilby Coleman. "I knew that justice would prevail. Those were the very points we went to the Supreme Court on—a total lack of sufficient evidence. I've never thought he did it, and I've never, ever thought the state proved he did it."[133]

Keller's aunt, Hyta Mederer, described the news of Owens's decision as a "'glorious day' with people 'pouring in' from everywhere. 'He's been in federal court since September 13, 1984, and we had hoped so much that he would be cleared before his mother, Russell, died, but she died on November 4, 1984. People have asked if it isn't time for his parole, but we didn't want him paroled, we wanted him cleared.'"[134]

Sonia, Keller's wife, "said her husband was in shock when she telephoned him Saturday morning to tell him of the reversal. 'He's very excited and looking forward to coming home,' she said. 'I feel like we finally got a fair shake.'"[135]

On the other side, feelings were equally intense. "I think it's the most ridiculous thing I ever heard of," said James Hanks. "He was found guilty. I guess people with money are going to rule the world. If you're a poor man, you can't get out, but if you've got money, you can work your way out through the courts. He'll be out on the streets and kill somebody else. There's no doubt in my mind he's guilty."[136]

Hellen's brothers expressed their bitterness. Doc Griffin said, "I knew he was going to get out sometime, but it's a shame our judicial system has turned out the way it has." Herman Griffin, Hellen's twin, said, "I know d*** well he was guilty. Everybody in the world knows he's guilty. The b****** stayed in there longer than I ever thought he would."[137]

Questioned by a reporter, police captain Charlie Spray said he was "very concerned" by Owens's ruling. "So far as the conduct or alleged misconduct that the courts are quoting, under the circumstances as they were at the time, I would do the same thing again," Spray said.

"I'm not sorry for it at all. I would do it again, and I think the community at large feels the same way."[138]

Lieutenant Billy Selph echoed Spray's feelings, stating that he was "very unhappy" with the ruling and confirming that he would not do things any differently if he had it to do over again. "All I can say is we worked the case as thoroughly as we could work it," Selph said. "We presented all the evidence in court to the twelve jurors here in Lowndes County. They made the decision and they found him guilty."[139]

Members of the jury that found Wilcox guilty were upset as well. Speaking on the condition of anonymity, two agreed to speak to a reporter.

> *"I feel strongly about it," one juror said. "I feel this strongly about it: I will never again sit on a jury of that type because my time was wasted. My time was absolutely wasted. I was locked up for two weeks. We heard every word of the evidence and we made a decision. Now, four years later a federal judge who's only read portions of it comes along and reverses the decision made by the jury and says there wasn't sufficient evidence to convict him. But if somebody comes along and confesses, you'll never convince me he didn't kill her. I didn't vote guilty on a whim."*[140]

A second juror said,

> *"I did have reasonable doubts until Keller Wilcox and his daddy testified, and that's what took all the doubt away from me. They weren't telling the truth, and that's all there was to it. Their stories didn't add up. Their timing didn't add up. Nothing they had to say sounded like the truth.*
>
> *I personally don't think I'd ever like to serve on a jury again. [Judge Owens] said we were incompetent and weren't able to reach a fair decision. Also, after the trial [Wilcox] was not allowed to be released on bond, so evidently all the state judges couldn't reach a fair decision either. Evidently, if they hadn't felt he was guilty too, he would have been out on bond."*[141]

A man-on-the-street "People Poll" by the *Daily Times* seemed to indicate a number of uninvolved local citizens disagreed with Owens's decision as well. In response to the question, "What do you think of the federal judge overturning the murder conviction of Keller Wilcox?" Earl Carpenter, a post office clerk, replied, "I don't think he should have done it. Wilcox was convicted by the jury and it should stand." Faye Simmons, a bookkeeper, said, "I don't think it was right. The jury found him guilty. I don't think it was fair." Howard Slocomb, a second-year law student at Mercer University, opined, "I don't think the federal judge should be able to overturn the jury's finding of fact. The jury sees the witnesses and can tell if they're telling the truth or not." Three others interviewed expressed similar opinions.[142]

On Monday, December 30, 1985, the last day on which Owens said he'd accept appeals to his decision to release Keller Wilcox on bail, Georgia Attorney General Mike Bowers's office filed a motion in opposition. In announcing that the state intended to appeal Owens's ruling, the attorney general's office pointed out that under federal guidelines, bail would not normally be granted unless there were "extraordinary circumstances" to justify Wilcox's release. "Petitioner has demonstrated absolutely no exceptional circumstances," the state maintained, hence his release on bail was not warranted. Owens rejected the motion. [143]

Keller was brought to the federal courthouse in Macon, where Judge Owens formally ordered him released on a $50,000 bond pending the state's appeal of Owens's ruling. "'I'm not bitter,' Wilcox said shortly after changing from his white prison uniform into a plaid shirt, khaki pants and a blue Izod sweater on the second floor of the federal courthouse here," the *Atlanta Constitution* reported. "I'm just glad to have reached this point in the journey." His wife, Sonia, described herself as "elated." "I sort of have to pinch myself to make sure it's real."[144] According to family members, Keller and Sonia left "on a trip to an undisclosed location." Foxy Wilcox observed, "They've been separated longer than they've been married. I hope they stay gone six months or a year."[145]

Chapter 26

The Second Life of Keller Wilcox[a]

On December 31, 1985, Keller Wilcox was back in Valdosta, for the moment a free man. Interviewed by a reporter for an Atlanta newspaper, he indicated that he intended to stay. "I'm glad to be back," Wilcox said. "I plan to stay here full time.... I knew all along that I was innocent of the crimes I was charged with. I knew the truth was going to come out. I just didn't know how long it would take." He said he planned "to spend his time getting reacquainted with his wife and family members."[146]

Lamar Cole, asked for a comment, noted, "The judge does not indicate he thinks Mr. Wilcox is innocent. He just doesn't agree with the jury that the case was clearly proven."

Reacting to this and similar comments circulating among the public, Keller indicated that he hoped to "better inform" Valdosta residents "about the flaws in the state's case against him by publishing Owens's seventy-two-page ruling" in the local *Daily Times*.[147] Several days later a six-inch-by-seven-inch display advertisement appeared in the paper, announcing that the decision would be published on January 6th.

Printed in miniscule type and occupying four full six-column pages, Owens's decision was preceded by an introduction from Wilby Coleman:

> *There has been speculation throughout the community as to the meaning and the validity of the decision of Judge Wilbur D. Owens, District Court Judge, in the Habeas Corpus case of Wilcox vs. Ford. There have*

---

[a] "The Second Life of Keller Wilcox" was the title of an article by James Dodson in the November 1986 issue of *Southern* magazine.

> *been street polls as to the rightness or wrongness of the Judge's decision. All of these opinions have been voiced without any idea as to what the facts were found to be and what the opinion says.*
>
> *The family and friends of Keller Wilcox have decided to publish the word-for-word opinion issued by Judge Owens. This is done at some expense and sacrifice. We trust that some will see the investigators at work as they coerced frightened witnesses into saying what the officers demanded that they say, or else suffer a dire variety of terrible retribution.*
>
> *We hope that some will understand this decision and recall that there is a Constitution in these great United States, which protects us all against penal servitude for crimes of which we are accused, but which the state fails to prove us guilty of, with or without coerced testimony.*
>
> *The District Attorney has made a statement to the press that Judge Owens did not find Keller Wilcox innocent. It is not necessary for Judge Owens to make such a finding, for the United States Constitution makes this finding. We hope that all who read this decision will remember that under the Constitution, as opposed to that of Russia, for example, we are innocent unless we are proven to be guilty. This is the very keystone of this nation and our way of life. Let us now bear it in mind.*[148]

The statement was signed by Wilby Coleman. It cost the family two thousand dollars to run it in the paper, nearly four months of Hellen Hanks's salary when she was employed at Wilcox Advertising.

The decision to publish Owens's ruling may have done more harm than good, prompting "shock and outrage" and "fresh outpourings of anger among jurors in the case, law enforcement officers and family members of the victim." Wilby Coleman, speaking to a reporter for the *Atlanta Journal-Constitution*, conceded that "the community is not jubilant over the decision."[149]

Jurors seemed to feel as if salt had been rubbed in their wounds. James E. Hendricks said he felt like Judge Owens was "telling him that I don't have enough sense to serve on a jury." He especially objected to the passage "in Owens's ruling in which the judge held that it 'insults rational thought' to convict Wilcox of murder based on the testimony of the state's key witness, Ed Wrentz.... 'Apparently Judge Owens is the only rational person in the state of Georgia,' said Hendricks." Frances Mays, another member of the jury panel, asked, "Why do we need a jury of twelve people when a judge is going to make all the decisions? I'm not ashamed of the verdict. I felt like it was a good verdict and [Wilcox] received a fair trial."[150]

Foxy Wilcox "said that running the opinion in the newspaper may have 'produced a few converts,' but some Valdostans will always think his son should have remained in prison. 'I just figure that there will always be people who are going to say something nasty. There's no use in trying to turn these people around.'"[151]

Based on their public statements, both Foxy and Wilby Coleman had seriously underestimated the degree of ill feeling resulting from Owens's ruling and its publication in the local paper. By the end of the month a petition calling for Owens's impeachment was circulating in several south Georgia counties. Addressed to the United States House of Representatives, it read (in part),

> *Let it be known, the People of the State of Georgia have been deprived of the use of Amendment 1, Amendment 6 and Amendment 14, Section 1 of the Constitution of the United States by the Middle District of Georgia Judge Wilbur Owens, on the release of E. K. Wilcox, Jr. for reason of reasonable doubt. Thereby we the Citizens of the United States of America demand Immediate Impeachment of Judge Wilbur Owens, Middle District of Georgia.*

Echols County Sheriff Charles Carter, who had a copy of the petition at his office, said that in the first day and a half since it was drawn up, some forty-seven people had come by to sign it.[152]

In February, "a Lowndes County grand jury...accused federal judges of 'callous disregard for the rights of crime victims and their families,' and asked for legislation to end lifetime appointment of the judges.... 'These decisions were made by men far removed from "trial by jury" which has always been considered the backbone of our legal system. We feel that the work done by grand jurors, petit jurors, investigators and other law enforcement officials has been rendered useless by these decisions.'"[b,153]

Keller Wilcox may have returned to his hometown, but the town that he returned to was not the same one he left some four years earlier. He was now a marked man in the eyes of many, and even if the federal court system eventually upheld the nullification of his conviction, its decision would likely carry little weight in the court of public opinion. In his absence, his mother had died, making Keller's wife, Sonia, her executor. Wilcox Outdoor Advertising had been sold. His father, Foxy, now in his late seventies, technically remained under indictment for his involvement in Hellen Hanks's murder. Given the series of events in Keller's case, however, it was unlikely that Foxy would ever face a jury.

The media had closely followed the discovery of Hellen Hanks's body, the investigation, the trial, and the appeals. With Keller now free and the strong possibility that he would not be retried, the ongoing saga had taken a fresh turn. Recognizing a good story, in the late spring of 1986 the editors of the newly inaugurated *Southern* magazine dispatched James Dodson to Valdosta to do a feature on this novel turn of events. Titled "The Second Life of Keller Wilcox," it ran as the lead article in November 1986, the second issue of the magazine.[154] Dodson, in his early thirties, had written extensively on Georgia topics. Being about Keller's age and having some experience in writing crime-related stories, he was a good choice for the assignment.[c]

---

[b] In addition to Judge Owens's overturning Keller Wilcox's conviction, the grand jury was angry about another December 1985 decision by the US Eleventh Circuit Court of Appeals that overturned verdicts in the horrific 1974 murders of six members of the Alday family in Donaldsonville, Georgia.

[c] *Southern* magazine, a glossy and heavily illustrated magazine featuring all things Southern, would last only about three years. During its short life it featured articles by a number of well-known and talented writers of the South, including many who had written for the Atlanta newspapers. The magazine's

The double-spread first pages of Dodson's article featured a large color photo of Keller, his arms crossed and clad in a plaid short-sleeved madras shirt, standing in front of a columned mansion and gazing off to the east in the direction of the rising sun. "Keller Wilcox ponders his future before a Valdosta landmark," the caption read. "Can he go home again?" The article was thoughtfully written and overall neutral in its outlook. Dodson described Keller as "a youthfully handsome man of thirty-four with sober hazel eyes and blondish neatly-barbered hair." His wife, Sonia, was depicted as "a thoughtful, no-nonsense woman." A photo of the two, standing in front of an expanse of green grass, was captioned, "After four and a half lost years, Keller and Sonia Wilcox simply want to pick up the pieces."

Most of the article was devoted to the details of Hellen Hanks's disappearance, the discovery of her body, and the subsequent trials and appeals. Beyond all this, Dodson focused on the community's reaction to Keller's return. An interview with a man who'd seen Keller in a downtown restaurant was revealing:

> *A local man, who admitted he had only vaguely known "the boy" accused of murdering Hellen Hanks almost fifteen years ago, lit a cigarette and stood beneath the shade of an awning on Main Street, watching Keller Wilcox cross through the gauzy light toward the bank.*
>
> *"He may be out," the observer commented narrowly, leaking smoke slowly through his nostrils, "but in my view the only reason he's walking the streets of Valdosta today is because of one thing and one thing only: his daddy's money."*
>
> *The man thumbed his cigarette to the pavement and ground it with his heel. "You know," he said solemnly, "that murder trial of his was*

---

founding editor was Linton Weeks. According to Weeks's biography on npr.org, *Southern* magazine "was bought—and crushed—in 1989 by Time-Warner" (www.npr.org/people/95608292/linton-weeks; Accessed July 29, 2017). James Dodson, the author of the article on Keller Wilcox, was interviewed by telephone on August 4, 2017.

said to be the most famous ever took place in south Georgia." He glanced again at the bank, but Wilcox had vanished inside. "People then thought he done what they said he done. Most of 'em, I'd wager, feel he done it. Killed that girl. But now here he is back, walking around as free as he pleases. Is that right? It's hard to say. People here will be decent to him, I expect—he's one of their own, after all. But don't ask them to forgive and forget what that judge in Macon done. This here was Valdosta business. Most folks got damn good memories—they seen them keys that convicted him. They heard about chopping off the young woman's legs...."

The observer allowed a tender pause and ticked his cheek meaningfully. "That boy," he announced with formal gravity, patting his shirt pocket for another smoke, "may pick up his life again, but it won't be the same for him. Never."

Equally revealing was Dodson's conversation with Keller. He said he wanted to stay in Valdosta and "was thinking of starting some kind of small business."

"People will come back to us once they've had time to reflect on everything, I feel sure," Keller said quietly. "And those that don't, well, nothing could change their minds. People believe what they want to believe. The thing that troubles me is, we may never know what really happened to Hellen Hanks. I lost four years of my life—and almost everything I have—because of poor police work. The judges in Atlanta might still see fit to send me back to prison. I don't know how it will turn out. All I know is I have my freedom again, my life. I'm grateful for that. I try not to be bitter. But it's time to go on."

Dodson observed: "You can overturn a murder conviction in court, but not in some people's minds."

Chapter 27

The End of the Road

Speaking to the Valdosta Kiwanis Club in the mid-spring of 1986, Assistant Attorney General Harrison Kohler said the state's appeal of Keller Wilcox's case would be his office's final involvement in the matter. "The appeal is pending and if we lose on the appeal the case will be over as far as we at the Attorney General's office are concerned."[155] This was to be the end of the road. It would be all or nothing for both sides. If Judge Owens's ruling were upheld, the practical outcome would be freedom for Keller. If his ruling were overturned, Keller would be facing decades behind bars.

The months passed quietly. Keller and Sonia kept a low profile, avoiding most of the social life that otherwise would have been the norm for a young married couple from prominent families. Keller found a job working with Georgia Petroleum in Valdosta.[156] In mid-October, news reports brought word that the federal Eleventh US Circuit Court of Appeals would hear arguments on the state's appeal on November 5th. The hearing would be held in Atlanta in front of a three-judge panel.

Presenting the state's case, Assistant Attorney General William Hill "said that Owens erred when he discounted [Ed] Wrentz's testimony, and asked the court to reverse and vacate Owens's ruling." Hill also said that Owens "abused his discretion" by granting Wilcox's release on a $50,000 bond. He asked the court to vacate this order as well.[157]

Speaking on behalf of his client, Bobby Lee Cook "argued that the 'completely barbarous' police interrogation of Wrentz and other witnesses was outrageous and proved that authorities were 'going to develop a case against Keller Wilcox one way or another.'" Even without Wrentz's "unbelievable" testimony, Wilby Coleman argued that "the remaining evidence implicating Wilcox in the slaying" was circumstantial and failed to prove he committed the murder.[158]

Foxy and Keller Wilcox attended the hearing, as did David Hanks, the victim's son. They sat on opposite sides of the courtroom. The panel of judges gave no indication as to when they would issue a ruling.

Five more months passed. On Friday, April 3, 1987, the court of appeals overturned Owens's ruling that the evidence was insufficient to convict Keller Wilcox on both criminal charges and reversed his order granting bail. In a scathing decision that addressed each of the points of the appeal, the court held that "the evidence presented by the State was clearly sufficient to support Wilcox's conviction for both murder and unlawful concealment of death."

In regard to Ed Wrentz's testimony, the court stated,

> *While Wrentz's testimony was to some extent confused and self-contradicting, we find that the testimony he gave on direct examination is not at odds with ordinary common sense or physically impossible under the laws of nature. The account of events given by Wrentz very well could have occurred. More than that, many of the aspects of his testimony are corroborated by other evidence, such as the indications of dismemberment, the fact that it rained the night of August 31st, and the description of the burial site. Furthermore, Wrentz's testimony as to the time of day the burial took place is consistent with the two periods of time during the day for which Wilcox, Jr. and Sr. were unaccounted for except by their own testimony.*

Addressing the issue of the harsh interrogation of suspects, the court ruled,

> *The police misconduct here, while not commendable, is not so extreme that it violates a sense of "fundamental fairness, shocking to universal justice" as far as Wilcox's constitutional rights are concerned. Nor do we find this case presents "the rarest and most egregious circumstances" which might justify finding that Wilcox's due process rights were violated.... Our review of the tapes and transcripts does not indicate any evidence of physical abuse or threats or improper inducements or promises in exchange for a statement implicating the defendant.*

The court concluded "that Wilcox did receive a fundamentally fair trial in spite of any government misconduct that might have occurred."

In reversing Keller's release on bail, the court noted that Judge Owens's finding that Keller would have "a likelihood of success on appeal was in error." He should not have been released.

News of the federal court's affirmation of Wilcox's conviction and the rescinding of his bail sent shock waves through the community. Contacted a few hours after the ruling was released, Wilby Coleman said he had not seen it, but commented, "There's no question but that we'll continue to appeal it," next to the United States Supreme Court. Keller was unavailable for comment. His whereabouts were unknown.[159]

Asked for his opinion on when Keller might have to return to prison, Assistant Attorney General Hill said,

> *Attorneys for Wilcox will probably attempt to keep the order in the appeals court in Atlanta in an effort to keep the order from reaching Judge Owens, which would then mandate Wilcox's immediate return to jail. "The lawyers have seven days in which to file a motion to stay the mandate," Hill said. "They have three options. They can file a petition for a rehearing before the three-judge panel. They can file a petition with a suggestion for a rehearing en banc, that is, ask all twelve 11th Circuit Court judges to take a look at the case. Or they can leave the 11th Circuit and begin a petition for certiorari to the [US] Supreme Court. It's like playing chess."*[160]

As word of the reversal spread, most seemed to believe justice had been served. A juror, speaking on the condition of anonymity, said he thought the court decision was "great." Hellen Hanks's brother, Herman Griffin, said, "I had a pretty sour view when [Wilcox] was turned loose by Owens. It kind of shattered my belief in the judicial system. Now that he's going back, it's restored my belief.... He knows he was guilty. I know, and the whole court system knew he was guilty. Why he was released, I'll never understand."[161]

Wilby Coleman "remained outraged." Speaking to a reporter, he said, "This is the first time I've ever heard where a federal court held that the testimony of one witness (Ed Wrentz) was sufficient to convict somebody, especially when that witness said, yes, he did have something to do with the burial, and no, he didn't have anything to do with the burial....The most distressing thing to me about it is, they have given police the stamp of approval to decide who they think is guilty and to go out and get a witness and force them to say what they want them to say." Coleman stated he would ask for a rehearing before all twelve judges of the Eleventh Circuit Court of Appeals.[162]

On May 11th, the court of appeals refused to rehear the case. The judges ruled that Keller "must return to prison immediately to serve the rest of his life sentence." "I think it's the right decision," Assistant Attorney General William Hill said. "There is no doubt. He is guilty of the murder."[163] The next afternoon, Keller turned himself in at the Lowndes County jail. The following morning he was transferred to the Georgia Diagnostic and Classification Prison near Jackson, Georgia, where he had begun his state prison sentence almost exactly four years earlier.

Keller may have been back in prison, but in Valdosta, the controversy continued. A large display ad in the May 20th issue of the *Daily Times* blared, "Listen To What They Say about Keller Wilcox. Guilty or Innocent?" Local radio station WZLS announced it "Will Air the Comments of the Defense Attorney, Wilby Coleman, and one of the Prosecuting Attorneys, Dwight May" on Sunday morning, May 24th. "You Be the Judge!" the ad suggested.

The June 1987 issue of the American Bar Association *Journal* featured an article titled "Judging the Judges," written by an attorney serving as a federal law clerk in the Western District of Pennsylvania.[164] Based on federal appellate decisions published in the Federal Register, among his findings, the author noted that "Judge Wilbur D. Owens, Jr. of the Middle District of Georgia, with a 7–16 record, had the lowest affirmance-reversal record." In other words, in the timeframe surveyed, Owens was said to have more reversals of his decisions than any other federal district court judge in the nation. The *Valdosta Daily*

Times dutifully reported the study on June 26, 1987, under the headline "Journal Rates Owens Last Among Judges," noting in the process that his ruling throwing out Keller Wilcox's conviction had been overturned. The paper also reported that in its upcoming August 1987 issue, the *Journal* planned to print a number of letters criticizing the June article, including a response from Judge Owens.[165]

Owens's letter in response to the *Journal*'s June article was venomous and menacing: "I demand that the American Bar Association and the Board of Editors of the *ABA Journal* immediately and publicly retract the false, malicious intentionally libelous opinions expressed as to this judge and publish the same with prominence equal to that given the libelous article, distributed so as to reach every member of the American Bar Association and the general public of these United States." Owens referred to the article's author as "a law clerk obviously possessed of no expertise qualifying him to judge the judges." In an expanded "Letters" section of its August issue, the *Journal* printed Owens's letter in full but did not issue a retraction.[166]

In early October 1987, Wilby Coleman filed an appeal asking the US Supreme Court to overturn his client's conviction, again citing "police misconduct concerning a witness and the state's failure to prove the guilt of Wilcox beyond a reasonable doubt." In response, the Georgia Attorney General's office filed a brief contending that "both issues had been disposed of properly by the 11th Federal Circuit Court of Appeals." Coleman expressed his confidence that the court would hear the appeal. Assistant Attorney General Hill opined, "Any lawyer telling you they will or will not hear the case does not know what he's talking about."[167]

In a brief, three-line statement dated November 2, 1987, the Supreme Court refused to hear Keller Wilcox's appeal. "There is no appeal left," Wilby Coleman stated. Seemingly unwilling to admit the obvious, he said the decision "did not necessarily mean they agreed with the 11th Circuit Court of Appeals or Judge Owens's decision.

This was a small potato case to them when they are dealing with abortion and other major issues you see in the news."[168]

Small potatoes or not, the decision meant that Keller Wilcox, now back in the Rutledge Correctional Institution in Columbus, Georgia, was facing the very real prospect of spending the rest of his life in prison.

Chapter 28

The Long Years

On February 22, 1989, Sonia Wilcox filed for divorce from Keller. Citing the fact that they had "lived in a bona fide state of separation" since May 12, 1987, and alleging that the marriage was "irretrievably broken," she asked the court to award her "an equitable division of all property acquired during the marital relationship."

Though perhaps not unexpected, it was a blow to Keller. In February 1982, less than a month after his conviction, he had given Sonia full power of attorney over all of his affairs.[a] After Keller's mother's death, he and Sonia served as joint trustees of the trust set up in the name of F. K. Wilcox Sr. Since Keller had been imprisoned for most of their marriage, it was Sonia who had managed his affairs and assisted his elderly parents with theirs. In the petition for divorce, Sonia noted "that she and the defendant (i.e., Keller) have acquired considerable properties during their marriage; that plaintiff (i.e., Sonia) has assisted the defendant in acquiring the properties; that they were not only partners in marriage, but in the accumulation of properties." A long list of assets followed, mainly stocks, bonds, certificates of deposit, and brokerage and bank accounts.

In his response, crafted by his new attorney, John T. McTier, Keller responded "that it is not his desire that the marriage relationship of the parties be ended." But he also denied "that the mere fact that [the] plaintiff's name has been placed on various accounts or assets for the purpose of convenience and accommodation to [the] defendant causes equitable ownership of those assets to be joint and several," continuing

---

[a] This power of attorney was not revoked until August 15, 1994, more than five years after Keller and Sonia divorced.

"that most of the assets acquired by [the] defendant subsequent to the date of his marriage to the plaintiff were produced neither by the efforts of or investments by the plaintiff." To this he added "that the plaintiff has accumulated substantial assets in her own name and in her own right." Against those he was making no counterclaim. By early August, the matter had been quietly settled. The details of the final divorce decree, issued August 4, 1989, were not made public. They remain on file in Lowndes County, sealed under orders from Judge H. W. Lott.

Foxy Wilcox died on November 15, 1990. He had been in declining health. With his wife dead and his son in prison, he spent his last days in a local nursing home. There was some speculation, perhaps unfounded, that Foxy would make a deathbed confession, alleging that it was he who killed Hellen Hanks, thus opening the possibility of his son's release from prison. It was not beyond the realm of possibility. Judge Wilbur Owens, in his decision that freed Keller in late 1985, had suggested that Foxy could have been the murderer. It did not happen. His indictment for the concealment of Hellen Hanks's death, now nearly a decade old, was never brought to trial. Foxy's obituary was that of a prominent and successful man, recalling only his positive contributions to the community.

Despite his failed appeals and his sentence of life in prison, Keller Wilcox continued to assert his innocence, seeking parole at every opportunity. Hellen Hanks's family, kept abreast of any parole applications via notifications from the State Board of Pardons and Paroles, responded each time with their objections. A 1992 letter from Hellen's husband, James Hanks, recounted the devastating effect on his family, reading in part,

> *Just the day before [Hellen disappeared], we were a happy family of five; three children in school, two working parents, and a new home. On that one day I lost nearly everything I had. I had to instantly become both mother and father to children who did not know what happened to their mother. And I had no explanation for them. Because Keller Wilcox and his father conspired to hide Hellen's body, there was no evidence of her death.*

> *My sole income was all we had to survive on. We had no insurance and no social security paid because of this concealment. Hellen had even ordered new living room furniture several weeks before that was soon delivered with a balance owed. Because of the questions surrounding Hellen's disappearance the local authorities even tried to take my children from me. So, you see, I not only lost the woman I loved and cared so deeply for, I also lost half our family income and the mother of my children who I needed with me to help raise and guide them.*[169]

Wilcox's parole was denied.

In late June 1993, Keller's application was once again before the parole board for the fourth hearing since the Eleventh Circuit Court of Appeals sent him back to prison six years earlier. This time was different in that the former sheriff of Lowndes County, Robert Carter, and the county's new sheriff, Ashley Paulk, both attended the parole board hearing in Atlanta at the request of attorney John McTier. Both testified in support of Keller's release from prison on parole. The public became aware of this in December 1993 when the news was revealed in a front-page article in the *Daily Times*.[170] Paulk's initial explanation as to why he testified seemed to fall flat, leading to several letters to the editor condemning both Carter and Paulk. These were published on the same day that the paper's editor printed the text of a question-and-answer interview with Paulk.[171]

Admitting that he'd known "Keller all his life," Paulk said he supported parole because he did not consider him to be a threat to the community. One of the letters to the editor opined, "Mr. Carter and Mr. Paulk I say to both of you, Keller Wilcox may not pose a threat to society but he sure posed a threat to Mrs. Hanks and he should stay right where he is until he is dead. At least when he dies, the state of Georgia will furnish a 'box' large enough so that his body won't have to be mutilated in order for him to fit into it." In another letter, Hellen's three children lambasted Paulk, saying, "In our opinion, your actions in support of your friend Keller Wilcox are a disgrace to the people of Lowndes County, to your Office and to justice."[172] Wilcox's parole was denied for a fourth time.

Several years passed without any progress toward release. In late 2003 or early 2004, Keller retained the Atlanta law firm of Balch & Bingham in an effort to secure his release. It was an expensive investment, reportedly costing a $100,000 fee.[173] Moreover, it was an ironic choice. One of the leading partners in the firm was Michael J. Bowers, the former Georgia attorney general whose office appealed Judge Owens's decision on a federal level and put Wilcox back in prison in 1987. The firm was well respected, however, and importantly, had excellent political connections, a definite plus when dealing with the parole board. Also, former DeKalb County District Attorney J. Thomas Morgan III joined Balch & Bingham as of February 2004, adding another well-connected name to an already impressive roster of attorneys. Less than three months earlier, Morgan had "vowed that he would never defend anyone accused of a violent crime."[174] Bowers and Morgan would be representing Keller in what would be his eighth attempt to gain parole.

In January 2004, Hellen Hanks's family was notified that the parole board would be giving "serious consideration" later in the spring to Keller's latest application. On April 6th, Bowers, Morgan, and Valdosta attorney John McTier submitted a long letter to the board requesting Keller's release on parole, accompanied by more than a hundred letters of support. The crux of the attorneys' argument favoring parole was that their client was innocent, wrongly convicted of a crime that occurred decades earlier, "a crime that he adamantly contends he did not commit." The letter continued,

> *Last month we advised our client that if he were guilty of the charge it would be in his best interest to confess to his crimes and show remorse for his actions. We had been advised that remorse is one of the considerations that the Board could factor in determining whether someone should be granted parole. Mr. Wilcox advised us that he could not admit to a crime for which he was not responsible, even if it meant foregoing his chance for parole.*

As further evidence of his innocence, the attorneys had their client take a polygraph exam which "concluded that Mr. Wilcox was telling the truth when he said he was not involved in the murder of Mrs. Hanks."

The remainder of the letter went on to reargue the defense's case presented at the 1982 trial. It alleged his "conviction was totally based on the testimony of two elderly witnesses" and that the Eleventh Circuit Court of Appeals decision sending Wilcox back to prison hinged on "a legal technicality." Perhaps hoping to score a home run with the board, the attorneys wrote, "Although presently we are only asking this Board to grant Mr. Wilcox a parole, there is more than sufficient evidence in this case to request the Board to consider a pardon for our client." Their client, the letter said, "has paid a debt to society for a crime he steadfastly maintains he did not commit and where there were outrageous police tactics used to secure critical testimony during the criminal investigation."

Accompanying the attorneys' letter were the polygraph report, more than a hundred letters of support, and a timeline of events in the case from 1972 through 2004. The timeline gave prominence to things that might cast doubt on Wilcox's conviction, including, for example, Judge Wilbur Owens's reasoning in overturning the jury verdict and a long excerpt of Ed Wrentz's 1981 interrogation by Charlie Spray juxtaposed with the fact that Spray had subsequently been convicted fifteen years later in 1996 for "stealing government property."[b]

More than ninety percent of the letters supporting parole were written between 1988 and 1990, a decade and a half before the current appeal. The majority of them had been collected by Sonia Wilcox prior

---

[b] Charlie Spray, who was Valdosta police chief when he resigned in 1995, was convicted by a Valdosta jury in 1996 for multiple counts of theft by taking of government property, specifically military surplus gear to be used in drug interdiction activity. Spray was sentenced to one year in prison and required to pay a $5,000 fine.

to her divorce from Keller and included many from prominent local citizens. Most were generic, commonly stating that the author had known Keller and his family for some time and thought he should be paroled. Everyone seemed to have forgotten the consequences of the crime, ignoring the victim and her family.

Bowers's and Morgan's efforts to free their client also included positive media coverage. Jim Wooten, a senior editorial writer and columnist for the *Atlanta Journal-Constitution*, wrote an editorial in the paper on April 20, 2004, urging Keller Wilcox's parole.[175] Echoing the attorney's letter to the parole board, Wooten said,

> *To this day, Wilcox, who has served twenty-one years of a life prison sentence, swears he did not commit the murder. Two polygraph tests were administered, one two months after the disappearance and another last month. He passed the most recent one for certain and likely did the other as well.... Because the district attorney did not agree to the polygraph, the results were not allowed a at 1981* [sic] *trial, where Wilcox was convicted on circumstantial evidence and the testimony of two elderly black employees who may have been improperly coerced by Valdosta police officers, one of whom later went to prison for theft by taking.*

The editorial went on to describe Judge Owens's overturning the verdict and the alleged harsh interrogation of Wrentz and Marshall. In conclusion, Wooten wrote,

> *Whether he is, in fact, guilty now hardly seems worth revisiting. He has served twenty-one years, during which time he has been a model prisoner. While free when his conviction was being appealed, he never attempted to flee. Wilcox is now up for parole. He has been denied three times before. Former Attorney General Michael Bowers and former DeKalb District Attorney J. Tom Morgan are helping—the first time either has gone to bat for any prisoner.*

Again, no mention was made of the victim or her family.

Russell Spivey, Penny Hanks's husband and an assistant district attorney in Georgia's Oconee Judicial Circuit, had become the acting spokesman for the family. He responded to Wooten's editorial three days later.[176]

Through his money, Wilcox gave himself every legal advantage he could muster. After he killed my wife's mother, he literally buried the evidence. But for the sheer providence of a man plowing a field in just the right spot, his crime would still be undiscovered. His family is from "old money" in the Valdosta area, and he and his father had the financial means to hire the renowned Bobby Lee Cook to defend him at trial. And he still has the means to hire big guns...to handle his parole effort.... If a public battle of the polygraphs must be waged, then it should also be known that both Wrentz and Marshall were polygraphed at the time of the murder. The results showed they were being truthful about helping Wilcox dig a hole and bury Hanks's body.

The battle in the press continued. *The Macon Telegraph* and the *Valdosta Daily Times* each ran long articles reviewing the now three decades-old crime. There were letters to the editor, including one from Lamar Cole, now retired, that contained a harsh rebuke of Michael Bowers.[177] The Hanks family paid to run a recurring display ad with a grinning mugshot of Keller Wilcox juxtaposed with a photo of Hellen Hanks, her husband, and children taken shortly before her disappearance. The text of the ad read,

*He is coming up for parole in May; he is well represented—**again**. He wants to return to Valdosta to live. He has never admitted to his actions and shows no remorse. Do you want this **convicted killer** living in your community?*[c]

In mid-May, Tom Morgan approached *Atlanta Journal-Constitution* columnist Bill Torpy about doing a feature on Keller Wilcox, then an inmate at the Georgia State Prison in Reidsville. For some time Wilcox, now fifty-three years old, had been considered a minimum-security inmate and was living and working at the firehouse outside of the

---

[c] The ad was published on multiple occasions in the *Valdosta Daily Times* in April and May 2004. Emphasis as shown duplicates that of the ad.

prison gates. Morgan drove Torpy to Reidsville himself, filling the columnist in on the details of the case during the three-hour drive.[178] Torpy interviewed Wilcox without his attorney present. Dressed in his fireman's uniform, and now somewhat pudgy after years in prison, Wilcox sat with "his hands folded, his sad green eyes fixed in concentration. 'I want to go home, to live in my house,' he said. 'I'm ready to put an end to this travesty.'"[179] The article, while neutral in tone, seemed somewhat sympathetic to Wilcox's plight. A photo showed Keller, sitting on the rear of a fire engine, petting the firehouse dog. Interviewed later, Torpy described him as "polite" and "smart" but "reticent to say much of anything." He presented himself as "an innocent man in prison" but was unwilling to discuss the crime. Torpy had the impression that "he'd been well coached. He was smart enough to say nothing."[180]

The media publicity generated a deluge of mail to the parole board, much opposing Wilcox's release. A man from Hellen Hanks's hometown collected more than four hundred signatures asking the board to deny parole. J. David Miller, the Valdosta district attorney and successor to Lamar Cole, penned a detailed letter systematically countering the points in Bowers's and Morgan's letter. He pointed out that one of the letters they submitted in support of parole came from Hulyn Smith but did not have a return address. Smith was the magistrate judge who presided over the Wilcoxes' committal hearing shortly after their arrest in 1981. This omission, Miller noted, was due to the fact that Smith was himself a state prison inmate, at the time serving a sentence "for attempting to hire an undercover GBI hitman to murder the Sheriff of Lowndes County so that he could be Sheriff."[181]

On June 4th, the board denied Keller Wilcox's parole. A spokeswoman said "the board believed that there was 'clear and convincing' evidence of Wilcox's guilt. 'The board also leaned heavily on the inmate's lack of remorse and failure to acknowledge guilt in the crime.'" They set the next date for parole consideration as May 2011, seven years hence.[182]

Russell Spivey, speaking for the Hanks family, said, "We are glad the parole board wasn't bamboozled by the arguments presented by the Wilcox attorneys. It seems like they weren't willing to be an appeals court or accept the attorneys' assertion that, 'We think he is innocent and you should, too.'" John McTier said he believed "in Wilcox's innocence and was deeply disappointed by the decision." Michael Bowers and Tom Morgan were not immediately available for comment.[183]

Chapter 29

Wilcox Confesses?[a]

Seemingly undeterred by their failure earlier in the year to win their client's release on parole, in November 2004 Bowers and Morgan submitted another request asking the board to reconsider its denial. This time making no assertions about Wilcox's guilt or innocence, they proposed that he had simply served enough prison time to warrant release.

In support of this, the attorneys examined all of the inmates who were serving life sentences and who were granted parole by the board between January 1, 2000 and August 30, 2004. There were eighty-three in all, of whom seventy-three had served less time that Wilcox. "We have reviewed the public information regarding the persons granted parole and it reveals that the aggregate crimes and records of the vast majority of those released are more severe than [those of] Mr. Wilcox." They concluded "there cannot be a rational basis for keeping Mr. Wilcox incarcerated based on the severity of the crime while at the same time releasing individuals who committed multiple felonies at the time of the murder; inmates with prior felony convictions; and inmates with greater security status and multiple disciplinary reports." The parole board rejected Bowers's and Morgan's request, but did move the next time for consideration of Keller's release from May 2011 to May 2008.

Three more years passed. In late November 2007, Hellen Hanks's family was notified by the Board of Pardons and Paroles that Keller Wilcox would be once again considered for release the following

---

[a] The title of this chapter is taken from the front-page headline of the *Valdosta Daily Times* on December 5, 2007. The question mark was part of the headline, expressing the paper's skepticism over the "confession."

month. The family was given less than two weeks' notice to submit comments. Hellen's brother, Steve Griffin, ran an ad in the Valdosta newspaper inviting the public to submit their objections to the parole board. Kevin Sumner, who'd collected hundreds of signatures opposing parole in 2004, began another petition. The *Daily Times* featured a long front-page article on the developments, but the reasons for moving up the potential parole date remained a mystery. In a December 4th editorial titled "Another Strange Twist," the *Daily Times* hinted at possible new developments in the case. "Our question is, why now? Why another parole hearing only three years after the last one," the editorialist asked. "Is it so, as one Hanks family member told the *Valdosta Daily Times*, that Wilcox can be released in time for the holidays? Or is there some other reason? Perhaps the answer to these questions will come this week. Perhaps it will be another defining chapter in the long, strange, sad journey of this case."[184]

The headline on the next morning's edition of the *Daily Times* read "Wilcox Confesses?" with the subheading "Letter to parole board contains admission of guilt." The paper had obtained a copy of a letter to the board dated July 11, 2006, nearly seventeen months earlier, in which Keller Wilcox admitted culpability in Hellen Hanks's death. According to the paper's account, the letter had been obtained by a "relative of Hanks" via an Open Records Act request submitted to the Office of Victim Services, a unit of the state Department of Corrections. As communications to the parole board were considered confidential, the letter and its contents had not been passed on to the family. Wilcox wrote to the board,

> *Dear Members of the Board:*
>
> *I want to acknowledge and accept responsibility for the death of Helen* [sic] *Hanks on August 31, 1972. Ms. Hanks was my father's secretary. We got into an argument and I lost my temper. I did not mean to hurt her. There was never a sexual assault or anything like that. I was scared and told my dad what happened. I was working for my dad at that time.*

I was not present when Ms. Hanks' body was buried in the field.

I am deeply regretful for the pain and suffering we have caused Ms. Hanks' family as a result of my actions on that afternoon. All the many years since that fateful afternoon I have tried to avoid bringing shame and embarrassment to my family by not admitting my responsibility. I am now 55 years old. It has been 34 years since Ms. Hanks' death. Now all my family members are deceased. Had I accepted the prosecutor's offer and admitted my guilt I would have been released from confinement many, many years ago.

I have been a model prisoner during my 23 plus years of confinement. I have been a trustee/firefighter for the last 12 years. I want to be a productive citizen, possibly a firefighter if I am released from confinement.

Thank you for your time considering this matter.

E. Keller Wilcox[185]

The "confession" appeared to many to be a cynical and self-serving document, designed solely to meet the parole board's stated criteria that two of the prime necessities for release were an inmate's acknowledgment of his actions and his expression of remorse. It was at odds with the known facts of the case. Since Keller's father, his last close family member, had been dead for nearly sixteen years, the claim of avoiding bringing "shame and embarrassment" to his family rang hollow. Furthermore, the confession itself directly implicated his father as an accessory to the crime.

Asked for his comment, former District Attorney Lamar Cole reacted strongly. "How can you cause bodily harm to someone after losing your temper if you don't mean to hurt them?" Cole asked. "Just because he has admitted his involvement, it does not mean that he has taken responsibility for what happened and owned up to all of his actions. Otherwise his letter would not include so many false statements. Admission says you did it, but confession says it all." The paper's account noted that "repeated attempts to reach Attorney Bowers in regard to the letter or the parole hearing have been unsuccessful."[186]

A few days later the parole board extended the deadline for the submission of comments to January 15, 2008, perhaps in reaction to the negative public response to Keller's letter. By January 13th, Keven Sumner from Brooks County had collected 1,123 signatures on a petition opposing parole.[187]

Nearly three months passed without further news. On Friday, April 11, 2008, the state Board of Pardons and Parole announced that the decision had been reached that Keller Wilcox would be freed on parole in the near future. The conditions of his parole included the necessity of wearing an electronic monitoring device, a lifetime ban from Lowndes and Brooks counties, and a provision that he have no contact with Hellen Hanks's family members.

An editorial in the *Daily Times* a few days later referred to Wilcox's release after submitting his letter of confession as "A Mockery of Justice":

> *Throughout these events and through the years, Wilcox maintained he did not kill Hanks, until he wrote a 2006 letter to the parole board insinuating responsibility for the murder. While Wilcox was denied parole on several occasions in the past, the confession letter likely spurred the parole board's recent decision to release him.*
>
> *If the letter was the key to his release, it almost sounds like something from the Salem witch trials of centuries past: If a person were innocent, she would sink and drown; if a witch she would float, live, and then be executed. With Wilcox, he could never win parole as long as he maintained his innocence, but once he confessed to having killed, he can be released. This makes a mockery of common sense, and seems to render a confession as not so much as a potential admission of guilt, but rather a ploy for freedom, whether guilty or innocent. It demeans our judicial system....*
>
> *The confession and the subsequent parole raise the questions: Did an innocent man confess in order to be freed after years of being wrongfully imprisoned? Or is a killer, who should remain in jail for his deeds, about to be free?*

On May 28, 2008, Keller Wilcox was released from the Georgia State Prison in Reidsville. Allowing for his sixteen months of freedom in 1985 to 1987, he had been incarcerated for twenty-five years. A news report that same day indicated that he would be living in Cobbtown, described as "a small town with friendly people" in rural Tatnall County, Georgia. The county's local weekly newspaper publisher "said rumors were the extent of the information regarding the Wilcox crime, and those rumors raised the question of whether or not Wilcox was guilty, a victim of a crime committed by his father."[188]

On May 30, 2017, the parole board denied Keller Wilcox's request for a commutation of his sentence. He was advised that he was eligible to reapply in eighteen months. A bit more than two weeks later, on June 16, 2017, the board removed Wilcox's ban from Lowndes and Brooks counties. He remains on parole.

Epilogue

Karma

If the course of our lives is decided by the Fates, then perhaps there is a hidden order in our existence. Or perhaps events occur randomly; we can never know. We can only speculate and wonder, puzzling over the "ifs" in our lives and the lives of others. In the case of Hellen Hanks's disappearance, *if* Fred Blanton had not decided to purchase Mildred Cothron's land, *if* he had chosen to do something other than clear it to plant crops, *if* those who buried the box containing her body had buried it only six inches deeper..., et cetera. If any of these actions had not taken place in the way that they did, this account would have ended with chapter 3. Dozens of lives would have taken a different course, some with empty sorrow, others with hidden secrets. Yet what happened, happened. The truth was known. Justice, however imperfect, was dispensed.

Appendix

I. A Chronological Timeline of Significant Events in the Hellen Hanks Murder Case

II. List of Individuals Who Had a Prominent Role in This Account

I. A Chronological Timeline of Significant Events in the Hellen Hanks Murder Case

1972:

- August 6: E. "Keller" Wilcox Jr. marries Jean King.
- August 29–31: E. K. ("Foxy") Wilcox Sr. and Keller Wilcox are in Atlanta for a business meeting.
- August 31: On returning to their business, Wilcox Outdoor Advertising, the Wilcoxes discover that the company secretary, Hellen Hanks, is missing.
- September through October: Investigations by local police agencies and the Georgia Bureau of investigation produce no leads as to Hanks's whereabouts. The case goes cold.

1979:

- June 12: Jean King Wilcox divorces Keller. Five months later she marries a friend of Keller's.

1980:

- October 25: Keller Wilcox marries for the second time to Sonia Lasseter.
- November 24: A farmer clearing new ground south of Valdosta discovers a box containing the remains of Hellen Hanks. The missing person case is now considered a homicide.
- November and December: An intense investigation begins, continuing into 1981.

1981:

- January through June: The investigation into Hellen Hanks's murder continues. The suspect list is narrowed.
- July 3: The owners of Wilcox Outdoor Advertising, Foxy and Keller Wilcox, as well as two black employees, Ed Wrentz and Lorenzo Marshall, are arrested. Keller Wilcox is charged with murder and concealing a death. The others are charged with concealing a death.

The Wilcoxes are released on bail and retain renowned defense attorney Bobby Lee Cook.

- July 24: At a committal hearing, the state presents its evidence. A judge rules that it is sufficient to warrant the proposed charges and binds the case over to a grand jury. Ed Wrentz, an important witness, is granted immunity.
- September 4: A Lowndes County Grand Jury indicts Keller Wilcox on charges of murder and concealing a death. Foxy Wilcox and Lorenzo Marshall are each indicted on charges of concealing a death and hindering apprehension and punishment of a criminal.
- September 18: The Wilcoxes and Marshall are formally arraigned.
- October through December: Pretrial hearings are held as both sides prepare their case. The trial is scheduled to begin on January 4, 1982. Keller Wilcox will be tried first.

1982:

- January 4–14: Keller Wilcox is tried and convicted of the murder of Hellen Hanks and of concealing her death. He is sentenced to life in prison plus twelve months, with his sentences to run consecutively.
- January 26: At an appeal bond hearing, Wilcox is denied bail and must remain in jail.
- June 18: At a hearing in front of federal District Court Judge Wilbur D. Owens, Wilcox is told that appeals in the federal court system must wait until he has exhausted his state court appeals.
- July 30: The Georgia Supreme Court denies Wilcox's release on bond.
- October 12: The Georgia Supreme Court hears arguments on Wilcox's appeal of his conviction.

1983:

- March 18: The Georgia Supreme Court affirms Wilcox's trial court conviction.
- March 30: The Georgia Supreme Court denies a rehearing of the case.
- May 10: His state court appeals denied, Wilcox is transferred from the Lowndes County jail to the Georgia State prison system.

- November: Alleging new evidence justifying throwing out Wilcox's conviction, his attorneys appeal to the Muscogee County, Georgia, Superior Court. Within days, the court rejects the appeal.

1984:

- April 25: The Georgia Supreme Court declines a review of the Muscogee County Superior Court decision, thus exhausting Wilcox's state court system appeals.

1985:

- May 16: The case is now back in federal Judge Wilbur Owens's court. A preliminary hearing is held in Macon, Georgia.
- July 9: A full hearing appealing Wilcox's conviction and the denial of his appeal bond on the federal level is held by Judge Owens in Macon.
- December 20: Judge Owens overturns Wilcox's conviction on multiple grounds. He says he will free Wilcox on bail unless the state presents convincing arguments against it.
- December 30: Wilcox is freed on $50,000 bail pending any appeals by the state. Wilcox returns to Valdosta.

1986:

- January thorough December: Wilcox remains in Valdosta, free on bail. The Georgia Attorney General Michael Bowers appeals the case to the Eleventh US Circuit Court of Appeals.
- November 5: The Eleventh Circuit Court of Appeals hears arguments from the state and Wilcox's attorneys over Judge Owens's ruling.

1987:

- April 3: The Eleventh Circuit Court of Appeals overturns Judge Owens's ruling. Wilcox is ordered back to prison.
- May 11: The court rejects a request for a rehearing on its ruling.
- May 12: Wilcox returns to the state prison system.
- November 2: The US Supreme Court declines a hearing on Wilcox's case, thus ending his court system appeals.

1989:

- August 4: Sonia Wilcox divorces Keller.

1990:

- November 15: Foxy Wilcox dies in a nursing home. His indictment for concealing Hellen Hank's death was never brought to trial.

1991–2003:

- Several appeals for Wilcox's release to Georgia's Board of Pardons and Paroles are unsuccessful.

2004:

- Wilcox mounts an aggressive attempt to gain parole, hiring former Attorney General Michael Bowers as lead attorney. Ironically, it was Bowers whose appeal on behalf of the state that put Wilcox back in prison in 1987.
- June 4: Wilcox is once again denied parole.

2006:

- July 11: Wilcox writes a letter to the parole board accepting responsibility for Hellen Hanks's death and expressing remorse. This document is kept secret.

2007:

- November: The state parole board announces that it will be considering Wilcox for parole in the near future; comments are requested. A family member files an Open Records request and is shocked to discover that Wilcox, who had steadily maintained his innocence, seems to have confessed to the crime.

2008:

- April 11: The parole board announces it will free Wilcox on parole in the near future.
- May 8: Wilcox is freed on parole. The conditions of his release include a ban from Lowndes and Brooks counties, electronic monitoring, and no contact with Hellen Hanks's family.

2017:

- Wilcox's ban from Lowndes and Brooks counties is lifted by the parole board. He can return home if he so chooses. The other conditions of his parole remain in effect.

II. List of Individuals Who Had a Prominent Role in This Account

Name	Brief Description of Role
Ronald Angel	GBI agent in charge of Major Crime Squad. Led investigation in to Hellen Hanks's disappearance in 1972.
Cora Arduengo	Hellen Hanks's friend. Testified for the state at trial.
Allen Loyce Arnold	Assistant police chief of Valdosta in 1972. Conducted initial investigation of Hanks's disappearance. Testified for both the state and for the defense at trial.
Dr. G. J. Austin	Keller Wilcox's godparent and cohost of the August 31, 1972, party at Ocean Pond. Testified for the defense at trial.
Ransom Manuel Bass	Police officer who responded to missing person report in 1972. Testified for the state at trial.
Michael Bennett	Edward Wrentz's court-appointed attorney.
Fred Blanton Jr.	Logger on whose land Hellen Hanks's remains were discovered in November 1980. Testified for the state at trial.
Michael J. Bowers	Georgia attorney general at time the state appealed Judge Wilber Owens's 1985 ruling on a federal court level. Later represented Keller Wilcox in attempts to win parole from prison.
Dr. Joseph L. Burton	Forensic pathologist. Testified for the defense at trial.
Sheriff Robert Carter	Sheriff at time of discovery of Hellen Hanks's remains.

Lamar Cole	District attorney in charge of prosecuting case against Keller Wilcox.
Wilby Coleman	Keller Wilcox's defense attorney during trials and appeals.
Bobby Lee Cook	Keller Wilcox's lead defense attorney during trial and appeals.
Leland Cothron	Member of the family who at one time had owned the land where Hellen Hanks's body was buried. Testified for the defense at trial.
Mildred Cothron	Owner of the land sold to Fred Blanton where Hellen Hanks's body was buried.
Edward Crow	One of the police officers present at crime scene burial site in 1980. Testified for the state at trial.
Jerry Davis	An employee of Wilcox Advertising in 1972. Testified for the state at trial.
D. J. Delancey	GBI agent who interviewed Keller Wilcox in 1972.
Gene Allen Deloach	Police officer who responded to missing person report in 1972. Testified for the state at trial.
William K. Devoir	Locksmith. Testified for the state at trial.
Dr. Park E. Dietz	A forensic psychiatrist who gave a report on the nature of Hellen Hanks's murder. He was not allowed to testify at trial.
James Dodson	Journalist who wrote an article on Keller Wilcox in 1986.
Dorothy Edwards	Hellen Hanks's best friend. Testified for the state at trial.
Cecil Franklin	A polygrapher for the GBI in 1972. Testified for the defense at trial.
John Wesley Goodman	Employee of Wilcox Advertising in 1972. Testified for the state at trial.
Herman Griffin	Hellen Hanks's twin brother.
Quinton "Doc" Griffin	Hellen Hanks's brother.
Steve Griffin	Hellen Hanks's brother.

Hellen Griffin Hanks	The murder victim. Disappeared on August 31, 1972. Her remains were discovered on November 24, 1980.
James Harold Hanks	Hellen Hanks's husband.
David H. Hanks	Hellen Hanks's son.
Lucy Hanks	Hellen Hanks's oldest daughter. Testified for the state at trial.
Daisy (Mrs. Garrard) Harrell	Keller Wilcox's great-aunt. Testified for defense at trial.
Van Hastings	Police officer who assisted in Keller Wilcox's arrest. Testified for the state at trial.
Leona Diane Head	Worked as secretary for Wilcox Advertising 1978–1980. Testified for the defense at the trial.
E. Cam Hickman	Lorenzo Marshall's court-appointed attorney.
William B. Hill	Georgia assistant attorney general. Was lead attorney on appealing Judge Wilbur Owen's 1985 ruling on a federal court level.
Dr. Harry Hollien	An expert in "phonetic sciences" who examined audiotapes for the defense.
Judge George A. Horkan	Judge who presided over the defendants' arraignment hearings.
Dr. James W. Howard	Director of the state branch crime lab in Moultrie, Georgia. Testified for state at trial.
Dr. Larry Howard	Director of the Georgia State Crime Lab. Testified for the state at trial.
Dr. Robert Jackson	Hellen Hanks's dentist. Identified victim's remains based on dental records. Testified for the state at trial.
Martha "Jean" King (Wilcox) Johannessen	Keller Wilcox's ex-wife. Married in 1972; divorced 1979. Subsequently married Neil Johannessen in 1980. Testified for the state at trial.

Carl Judge	Employee at Valdosta Municipal Airport whose duties included weather monitoring. Testified for the state at trial.
Dr. Ellis Kerley	Forensic anthropologist. Testified for the state at trial.
Martha A. King	Jean Johannessen's mother and Keller Wilcox's ex-mother-in-law. Testified for the state at trial.
Willard King	Jean Johannessen's father and Keller Wilcox's ex-father-in-law. Employee of Wilcox Advertising. Testified for the state at trial
John B. Lastinger	Officer of the Valdosta/Lowndes County Chamber of Commerce. Testified for defense at first bond hearing.
Charlene Levine	Certified interpreter for the deaf. Acted as interpreter for Sandra Williams's testimony at trial.
Judge Roy M. Lilly	Judge who presided over Keller Wilcox's trial.
Fran Lofton	A clerk at the Minit Mart next to Wilcox Advertising in 1972. Testified for the state at trial.
Herman Lyle	Retired FBI agent and friend of Keller Wilcox. Testified for the defense at trial.
Harry Lynch	Employee of Chemical Specialties, Inc., next to Wilcox Advertising in 1972. Testified for the state at trial.
Lorenzo Marshall	Employee of Wilcox Advertising in 1972. Allegedly helped bury box containing Hellen Hanks's body. Testified for the state at trial.
Dwight May	Assistant special prosecutor hired by Hanks family
Mary Alice May	Employee of Wilcox Advertising in 1971. Testified for the state at trial.

John T. McTier	Attorney who represented Keller Wilcox in his second divorce and subsequent parole attempts.
Hyta Mederer	Keller Wilcox's aunt and Foxy Wilcox's sister-in-law. Stepmother-in-law of Wilby Coleman.
J. Thomas Morgan III	Former DeKalb County district attorney. Represented Keller Wilcox in attempts to win parole from prison.
Doug Moss	Investigator for Bobby Lee Cook's law firm.
Judge Wilbur D. Owens Jr.	Federal district court judge who overturned Keller Wilcox's conviction and freed him on bond in December 1985.
Larry Oxford	GBI agent who interviewed Keller Wilcox in 1972. Testified for the state at trial.
Billy E. Register	Captain with the Valdosta Police Department. With Billy Selph, led the investigation after Hellen Hanks's remains were found. Testified for the defense at trial.
Kevin Riley	President of the Lamar Advertising Company, with which Wilcox Advertising executed a management agreement in August 1972. Testified for the defense at trial.
Ellis M. Rountree	Employee of Wilcox Advertising in 1972. Testified for the defense at trial.
Salem Franklin Scott	Man who purchased Wilcox Advertising's former truck. Testified for the state at trial.
Billy W. Selph	Officer with the Lowndes County Sheriff's Department. With Billy Register, led the investigation after Hellen Hanks's remains were found. Testified for the state at trial.
Arlie Smith	One of the police officers present at crime scene burial site in 1980. Testified for the state at trial.

Carl Smith	Employee of McGowan Funeral Home through 1972. Testified for the defense at trial.
Edward Smith	Employee of Wilcox Advertising in 1972. Testified for the defense at trial.
Judge Hulyn E. Smith	Magistrate judge who presided over the Wilcoxes' commitment hearing.
Penny Hanks Spivey	Hellen Hanks's youngest daughter.
Russell Spivey	Husband of Penny Hanks Spivey.
Charlie Spray	Police officer who assisted in the investigation of Hellen Hanks's murder.
Tommy Strom	Embalmer at McGowan Funeral Home 1970–1975. Testified for the defense at trial.
Bill Torpy	Journalist who wrote a 2004 feature newspaper article on Keller Wilcox.
Lamar Wansley	Cohost of August 31, 1972, party at Ocean Pond.
E. K. ("Foxy") Wilcox Sr.	Keller Wilcox's father, charged as an accessory to Hellen Hanks's murder.
E. Keller Wilcox Jr.	Defendant charged with the murder of Hellen G. Hanks.
Lota Wilcox	Keller Wilcox's aunt by marriage. Testified for the defense at trial.
Sonia P. Lasseter Wilcox	Keller Wilcox's second wife (1980–1989).
Carla Wilkerson	Employed for several months at Wilcox Advertising in 1981. Testified for the defense at trial.
Sandra Williams	Hellen Hanks's friend and hairdresser. Testified for the state at trial via a deaf/mute translator.
Virginia Wisenbaker	Guidence counselor at Valdosta High School. Testified at appeal bond hearing.
Jim Wooten	Journalist who wrote a 2004 editorial favoring Keller Wilcox's release on parole.

Edward Wrentz	Former employee of Wilcox Advertising. Allegedly helped bury box containing Hellen Hanks's body.
Donald M. Wright	Employee of Wilcox Advertising's Albany office. Testified for the state at trial.
John Wyatt ("Buddy") Yow Jr.	Keller Wilcox's first cousin. Testified for the defense at trial.

Author's Note and Acknowledgments

Writing this account of Hellen Hanks's murder, the subsequent investigation, trial, and appeals was not a simple task. It could not have been completed without assistance and input from numerous individuals, in addition to drawing upon the resources of several institutions. There was a plethora of data, including media reports, but the real heart of the factual information was found in the numerous legal records, transcripts, and evidence gathered during the investigation of the murder and as part of Keller Wilcox's hearings, trial, and appeals. Hearing and trial transcripts alone numbered in excess of 3,000 pages.

First, I must thank the family of Hellen Hanks for their assistance and making available to me their scrapbooks, correspondence, photos, and other memorabilia relating to her disappearance, the discovery of her remains, and to Keller Wilcox's trial and the appeals that followed. Without the kindness of David and Wynne Hanks and Russell and Penny Spivey, the task of writing this book would have been all the more difficult. I did not have the opportunity to meet Hellen Hanks's third child, Lucy. Tragically, she succumbed to cancer shortly after I began my research.

I thought it would be only fair if I made an effort to seek Keller Wilcox's input as well. I contacted him via mail and via a mutual acquaintance. He was aware that I was writing a book on Hellen Hanks's murder. Through the mutual acquaintance, he declined to accept my request for an interview.

Valdosta is a lovely city at the far edge of Georgia's coastal plain, its streets shaded by live oaks and pines, its people friendly and welcoming. During several trips there, I was fortunate to receive assistance and input from many individuals. One of my first stops in Valdosta was the Lowndes County Historical Society Museum, located in a hundred-year-old former Carnegie Library building near the heart of town. Donald Davis, the museum's director, and Harry Evans, in charge of

Special Collections and Research, were exceptionally helpful, assisting me in every way and allowing me to copy items from the museum's extensive files.

Lamar Cole, the now-retired former district attorney who led the state's prosecution in the Wilcox murder trial, was kind enough to sit down with me for a very long interview. His insights into the case were unique and vital to the story. Likewise, the current district attorney, Brad Shealy, who is most familiar with the Wilcox trial, offered excellent insights and allowed me to make copies of the photos introduced as evidence at the 1982 trial.

The staff of the Lowndes County Clerk of Court's office, especially LaToya Brown and Dede Wheeler, worked diligently to retrieve for me various records and evidence from the Wilcox hearings and trial. They made a room available in which I could study, copy, and photograph documents and exhibits. I also spoke with a number of other individuals in the Valdosta area who were willing to discuss the case with me. They showed me the lay of the land and helped guide me thorough the intricate social and political webs that are the hallmark of any small Southern city. For their input, I am grateful as well.

The library of Valdosta State University was the source of many of the older newspaper articles from the *Valdosta Daily Times.* Archive copies of the *Quitman Free Press* were reviewed at the Brooks County Courthouse, as were other records pertaining to marriage and divorce. A copy of the transcript of the 1982 trial of *State v. Wilcox* is located at the Georgia State Archives in Morrow, Georgia. It is archived there with other records of cases reviewed by the Georgia Supreme Court. The state archives were also the source of several other miscellaneous documents reviewed for this account. As always, the staff there was most knowledgeable and helpful.

I want to express my appreciation to Marc Jolley and the staff at Mercer University Press for their support and assistance to me over the past several years with this book and others. My muse, Laura Ashley, was her usual inspiring self, flogging me on as I waded through thousands of pages of documents in my quest to extract a cogent narrative.

Finally, I want to thank my family for their support and patience during the many hours devoted to the production of this book. As with every book I've written, I have learned much in the process. I came away with a new respect for the concept of the law and a new sense of understanding of how things actually work in the real world of the justice system. It was an interesting journey. For those who don't quite understand the Latin phrase *res ipsa loquitur*, I use this in a literal, as opposed to legal, sense.

Notes

[1] Trial transcript, *State v. Wilcox* (1982).

[2] The record is at times confusing with regard to the names of Elisha Kella Wilcox and his son and grandson. "Foxy" Wilcox is often referred to "E. K. Wilcox Jr." when his name appears in relationship to that of his father. His 1945 wedding announcement, for example, gives his name as "Ernest Keller Wilcox, Jr," while his 1990 obituary gives his name as "Ernest Keller Wilcox, Sr." His son, "Keller," born in 1951, is also named "Ernest Keller Wilcox Jr." After this date Foxy's name is generally given as E. K. Wilcox Sr. It may be that Foxy chose, legally or otherwise, to change his name from that of his father to more conventional spellings. The naming system used in this book follows that used in court proceedings, with Ernest Keller Wilcox Sr. known as "Foxy" and his son, Ernest Keller Wilcox Jr., known as "Keller."

[3] https://www.gabar.org/MemberSearchDetail.cfm?ID=NzU4NDAw (Accessed May 5, 2018)

[4] *Valdosta Daily Times*, November 17, 1990

[5] http://www.pbs.org/ladybird/shattereddreams/shattereddreams_report.html (Accessed April 8, 2018)

[6] *Tampa Bay Times*, September 20, 1981.

[7] Ibid.

[8] Trial transcript, *State v. Wilcox* (1982).

[9] Ibid.

[10] Ibid. See Defendant's Exhibit 73.

[11] Trial transcript, *State v. Wilcox* (1982).

[12] *Atlanta Journal-Constitution*, January 6, 1982.

[13] Trial transcript, *State v. Wilcox* (1982).

[14] *Valdosta Daily Times*, September 2, 1972.

[15] Trial transcript, *State v. Wilcox* (1982). See Defendant's Exhibit 2.

[16] Trial transcript, *State v. Wilcox* (1982).

[17] Ibid.

[18] *Valdosta Daily Times*, June 19, 1972.

[19] Ibid., October 3, 1972.

[20] *Quitman* (GA) *Free Press*, October 12, 1972.

[21] Trial transcript, *State v. Wilcox* (1982).

[22] Ibid.

[23] *Atlanta Constitution*, July 13, 1981.
[24] Interview with Penny Hanks Spivey, March 20, 2018.
[25] Ibid.
[26] David Hanks, email correspondence, April 9, 2018.
[27] Interview with Penny Hanks Spivey, March 20, 2018.
[28] Interview with Barbara Stratton, January 18, 2018.
[29] Interview with Penny Hanks Spivey, March 20, 2018.
[30] *Quitman* (GA) *Free Press,* September 9, 1972.
[31] Ibid., August 31, 1972.
[32] Ibid., October 5, 1972.
[33] *Marietta Journal,* September 21, 1973.
[34] *Augusta Chronicle*, July 28, 1973,
[35] *Marietta Journal,* July 29 and 30, 1973.
[36] *Brunswick* (GA) *News,* August 17, 1974.
[37] James Dodson, "The Second Life of Keller Wilcox," *Southern Magazine* (November 1986).
[38] Ibid.
[39] *Valdosta Daily Times*, March 13, 1980.
[40] Interview with Lamar Cole.
[41] James Dodson, "The Second Life of Keller Wilcox," *Southern Magazine* (November 1986).
[42] *Valdosta Daily Times*, November 25, 1981.
[43] Ibid.
[44] Trial transcript, *State v. Wilcox* (1982).
[45] Email correspondence with David Hanks, June 6 2018.
[46] Email correspondence with Penny Spivey, March 30, 2018
[47] *Valdosta Daily Times*, November 28, 1980.
[48] Ibid., November 30, 1980.
[49] Ibid., December 2, 1980.
[50] Trial transcript, *State v. Wilcox* (1982).
[51] *Valdosta Daily Times*, March 11, 1981.
[52] Ibid., April 3, 1981.
[53] Ibid.
[54] The events of Keller Wilcox's arrest are based on his testimony given at trial.
[55] *Valdosta Daily Times*, June 28, 1981.
[56] *Atlanta Constitution*, July 4, 1981.
[57] *Valdosta Daily Times*, July 4, 1981.

[58] Anthony Schmitz, "The Jazz Justice of Bobby Lee Cook," *Atlanta Weekly* (December 13, 1981).

[59] *Los Angeles Times*, July 30, 1986.

[60] Mark Curriden, "Bobby Lee Cook: Georgia Maverick," *ABA Journal* (March 1989).

[61] Interview with Lamar Cole, March 9, 2018.

[62] *Florida Times-Union* (Jacksonville), June 16, 1996.

[63] Unless otherwise referenced, the source of the information presented in the chapter, including quotes, is the transcript of the committal hearing held July 24, 1981, before Judge E. Hulyn Smith.

[64] Lowndes County Grand Jury Indictment, September 4, 1981.

[65] *Valdosta Daily Times*, July 25, 1981.

[66] Ibid., July 26, 1981.

[67] *Florida Times-Union* (Jacksonville), October 14, 1981.

[68] *Tampa Bay Times* (St. Petersburg), September 20, 1981.

[69] *Atlanta Constitution,* October 11, 1981.

[70] Letter: Park E. Dietz, MD, to Lamar Cole, September 27, 1981.

[71] Ibid.

[72] *Atlanta Constitution*, October 11, 1981.

[73] Ibid.

[74] *Florida Times-Union* (Jacksonville), October 12, 1981.

[75] Ibid., October 14, 1981.

[76] Hearing transcript, December 21, 1981.

[77] Ibid.

[78] Hearing transcript, December 30, 1981.

[79] *Valdosta Daily Times*, January 4, 1982.

[80] Ibid, January 5, 1982.

[81] *Atlanta Constitution*, January 6, 1982.

[82] Ibid.

[83] Ibid.

[84] Ibid.

[85] *Valdosta Daily Times*, January 10, 1982.

[86] Ibid.

[87] *Atlanta Constitution*, January 8, 1982.

[88] Ibid.

[89] Ibid.

[90] Ibid., January 11, 1982.

[91] *Valdosta Daily Times*, January 11, 1982

[92] Ibid., January 17, 1982.

[93] Ibid., January 12, 1982.

[94] Anthony Schmitz, "The Jazz Justice of Bobby Lee Cook," *Atlanta Weekly* (December 13, 1981).

[95] *McNabb v. United States*, 318 U.S. 332 (1943)

[96] *Atlanta Constitution*, January 15, 1982.

[97] *Valdosta Daily Times*, January 17, 1982.

[98] *Atlanta Constitution*, January 15, 1982.

[99] *Valdosta Daily Times*, January 17, 1982.

[100] *Atlanta Constitution*, January 15, 1982.

[101] *Valdosta Daily Times*, January 17, 1982.

[102] Ibid.

[103] Ibid.

[104] Ibid.

[105] *Florida Times-Union* (Jacksonville), January 17, 1982.

[106] *Valdosta Daily Times*, January 17, 1982.

[107] Ibid., January 11, 1982.

[108] Ibid., January 22, 1982.

[109] Ibid., January 21, 1982.

[110] Ibid., January 28, 1982; *Florida Times-Union* (Jacksonville), January 27, 1982.

[111] *Wilcox v. Carter*, 545 F. Supp. 1043 (1982)

[112] *Valdosta Daily Times*, June 19, 1982.

[113] Ibid., March 1, 1982.

[114] Ibid., June 18, 1982.

[115] R. Robin McDonald, "Bowers, Morgan Attempting to Free Killer in 1972 Murder," *Fulton County Daily Report*, May 5, 2004.

[116] Ibid., July 9, 1982.

[117] Ibid., July 16, 1982.

[118] Ibid., August 2, 1982.

[119] Ibid., October 13, 1982.

[120] *Atlanta Constitution*, October 13, 1982.

[121] *Valdosta Daily Times*, October 13, 1982.

[122] Ibid., March 21, 1983.

[123] Ibid., March 31, 1983.

[124] Ibid., November 2, 1983.

[125] Letter: Wilbur Owens to Mary B. Westmoreland, May 6, 1985.

[126] *Valdosta Daily Times*, May 16 and 17, 1985.

[127] Ibid., June 21, 1985.

[128] *Atlanta Constitution*, May 17, 1985.

[129] *Valdosta Daily Times*, July 10, 1985; *Atlanta Journal*, July 10, 1985.

[130] *Atlanta Journal-Constitution*, December 22, 1985.

[131] Ibid.

[132] Ibid.

[133] *Valdosta Daily Times*, December 22, 1985.

[134] Ibid.

[135] Ibid.

[136] Ibid.

[137] Ibid.

[138] Ibid., December 23, 1985.

[139] Ibid.

[140] Ibid.

[141] Ibid.

[142] Ibid., December 29, 1985.

[143] *Atlanta Journal*, December 31, 1985.

[144] *Atlanta Constitution*, December 31, 1985.

[145] *Valdosta Daily Times*, December 31, 1985.

[146] *Atlanta Journal-Constitution*, January 1, 1986.

[147] Ibid.

[148] *Valdosta Daily Times*, January 6, 1986.

[149] *Atlanta Journal-Constitution*, January 18, 1986.

[150] Ibid.

[151] Ibid.

[152] *Atlanta Journal*, January 30, 1986; *Valdosta Daily Times*, February 5, 1986.

[153] *Atlanta Journal-Constitution*, February 15, 1986.

[154] James Dodson, "The Second Life of Keller Wilcox," *Southern Magazine* (November 1986).

[155] *Valdosta Daily Times*, April 11, 1986.

[156] Letter: William J. Holland to Georgia Board of Pardons and Paroles, March 29, 2004.

[157] *Atlanta Constitution*, November 6, 1986.

[158] Ibid.

[159] *Valdosta Daily Times*, April 4, 1987.

[160] Ibid., April 5, 1987.

[161] Ibid.

[162] *Valdosta Daily Times*, April 5 and 6, 1987.

[163] *Florida Times-Union* (Jacksonville), May 12, 1987.

[164] Brian L. Weakland, "Judging the Judges," *ABA Journal* (June 1987).

[165] *Valdosta Daily Times*, June 26, 1987.

[166] "Letters," *ABA Journal* (August 1987).

[167] *Valdosta Daily Times*, October 14, 1987.

[168] Ibid., November 5, 1987.

[169] Letter: James H. Hanks to Members of the Georgia State Board of Pardons and Paroles. Undated but submitted in September 1992.

[170] *Valdosta Daily Times*, December 17, 1993.

[171] Ibid., January 9, 1994.

[172] Ibid.

[173] *Valdosta Daily Times*, March 21, 2008.

[174] R. Robin McDonald, "Bowers, Morgan Attempting to Free Killer in 1972 Murder" *Fulton County Daily Report*, May 5, 2004.

[175] *Atlanta Journal-Constitution*, April 20, 2004.

[176] Ibid., April 23, 2004.

[177] *Valdosta Daily Times*, April 30, 2004.

[178] Interview with Bill Torpy, August 22, 2018.

[179] *Atlanta Journal-Constitution*, May 23, 2004.

[180] Interview with Bill Torpy, August 22, 2018.

[181] Letter: J. David Miller to State Board of Pardons and Parole, May 21, 2004.

[182] *Atlanta Journal-Constitution*, June 5, 2004.

[183] Ibid.

[184] Ibid., December 4, 2007.

[185] Ibid., December 5, 2007.

[186] Ibid.

[187] Ibid., January 13, 2008.

[188] *Quitman* (GA) *Free Press*, May 28, 2008.

Index